In Praise of
Railroads and Clearcuts

"This is the story of the biggest land grant in American history, larger than 10 Connecticuts, to railroad companies and how the timber companies got hold of huge forests to clearcut. Jensen and Draffan point the way to returning these lands to their rightful owners – the American people who will preserve them for future generations. A revealing report of government giveaways and corporate perfidy and greed that motivates corrective action."

– Ralph Nader, Washington, D.C.

"Here at last is a book which documents in detail the abuses of public trust which have so scarred the wilderness legacy of our Pacific Northwest states, and which at the same time offers some hope for redressing and making right, at last, these ancient wrongs."

– Brock Evans, lifetime conservation activist and organizer for national environmental organizations.

"This book shows clearly how Congress has always had the authority to oversee the Northern Pacific land grants but it has rarely exercised it. Federal oversight to protect the public interest is even more essential today than 100 years ago."

– E. Kimbark MacColl, historian, Portland, Oregon.

"Ecosystem management will never be achieved in the Pacific Northwest until the checkerboard railroad lands are returned to their rightful owners – 'the American public!' Probably no other single event in this country has contributed more to the current Northwest forest crisis than the profit-driven harvest activities on the old railroad checkerboard lands."

> **– John Mumma,** U.S. Forest Service Regional Forester, Northern Region, 1988-1991.

"Railroads played such an important role in the making of the Pacific Northwest – far more than in other parts of the United States – that no one can hope to understand the modern region without comprehending the railroad impact on the land and its settlers."

> **– Carlos Schwantes,** Professor of History at the University of Idaho and author of *Railroad Signatures across the Pacific Northwest.*

"The saga of the nineteenth-century railroad barons is no closed chapter. The work of J.P. Morgan, who controlled the Northern Pacific Railroad and who defiantly proclaimed, 'I owe the public nothing,' lives on. Yet the abuses in the 1990s are not confiscatory rail tariffs but rather some of the world's most irresponsible logging practices in the spectacular watersheds of Montana, Idaho, and Washington. For the Northern Pacific has sold much of its munificent land subsidy — 40 million acres of the public's land — to big timber companies that operate in a regulatory vacuum. An 1864 railroad giveaway has become a modern forest-policy nightmare.

Railroads and Clearcuts makes the case that the timber companies are fully accountable to the public and that Congress can, and should, take decisive action. This valuable account is essential information for all those who want to see justice done in the deep woods of the northern tier."

> **– Charles F. Wilkinson,** Moses Lasky Professor of Law at the University of Colorado and author of *Crossing the Next Meridian – Land, Water and the Future of the West.*

RAILROADS AND CLEARCUTS

LEGACY OF CONGRESS'S
1864 NORTHERN PACIFIC RAILROAD LAND GRANT

RAILROADS AND CLEARCUTS

LEGACY OF CONGRESS'S
1864 NORTHERN PACIFIC RAILROAD LAND GRANT

DERRICK JENSEN AND GEORGE DRAFFAN

WITH JOHN OSBORN, M.D.

INLAND EMPIRE PUBLIC LANDS COUNCIL
SPOKANE, WASHINGTON

DISTRIBUTED BY KEOKEE CO. PUBLISHING, INC.
SANDPOINT, IDAHO

© 1995 Inland Empire Public Lands Council
P.O. Box 2174, Spokane, WA 99210
Phone: (509) 838-4912, Fax: (509) 838-5155
Internet: IEPLC@uwsa.spk.wa.us

Distributed by
Keokee Co. Publishing, Inc.
P.O. Box 722, Sandpoint, ID 83864
Phone: (208) 263-3573, Fax: (208) 263-4045

Printed on Springhill Incentive 100, a 100 percent recycled paper made from 100 percent old newspapers, magazines and catalogs de-inked without chlorine and manufactured in a closed-loop system which recovers and reuses water processed with the paper pulp. This paper is acid-free and has a shelf life of 200 years.

Printed with ecology conscious soy ink.

Publisher's Cataloging-in-Publication Data
Jensen, Derrick, 1960-
    Railroads and clearcuts : legacy of congress's 1864 northern pacific railroad land grant / by Derrick Jensen, George Draffan, John Osborn.
        xviii, 198 pages : ill.
ISBN: 1-879628-08-2

1. Railroad Land Grants — Pacific Northwest — History. 2. Forest Products Industry — Pacific Northwest. 3. Northern Pacific Railroad Company — History. 4. Forest Conservation — Pacific Northwest. I. Draffan, George. II. Osborn, John. III. Inland Empire Public Lands Council. IV. Title.
HE2791.N855R24   1995
333.16 — dc 20

CONTENTS

Figures

Tables

DEDICATION

"Those who cannot remember the past
are condemned to repeat it."
– Santayana

This book is dedicated to the people and ecosystems of the Pacific Northwest harmed by Congress's land-grant legacy and to future generations who will live with further forest destruction if we fail to remember the past.

– John Osborn, M.D.,
Inland Empire Public Lands Council

Quotes from the History of Congress's 1864 Northern Pacific Railroad Land Grant

1864

". . . Congress may, at any time, with due regard for the rights of said Northern Pacific Railroad Company, add to, alter, amend, or repeal this act."

– 1864 Northern Pacific Railroad Land Grant

1883

"I hate you. I hate you. I hate all the white people. You have taken away our land and made us outcasts, so I hate you."

– Chief Sitting Bull

1901

"I owe the public nothing."

– J.P. Morgan

1924

"The defaults of the Northern Pacific were numerous and flagrant, and the supplementary benefits allowed by the Government were many and lavish, but in the absence of action by Congress the courts and the administrative departments were and are without authority to consider the resulting equities, but have been forced to act as though the company had complied with every term of the grant, both in spirit and letter."

– President Calvin Coolidge, letter to Congress requesting an investigation of the Northern Pacific land grant.

1940

"Northern Pacific Railway grant lands in the Washington national forests total more than three-fourths of a million acres of checkerboard odd sections. This intermingled ownership decreases the value of the government land to community welfare simply because we find it impossible to work out effective plans for management under these circumstances."

> – **Henry Wallace**, President Franklin Delano Roosevelt's Agriculture Secretary.

1988

"If you look just at industry, you would say industry has overcut their lands, that they have removed their volumes too quickly, that they have created a hellacious hole or gap. I don't think anyone would disagree with that."

> – **Champion International**, regional planning manager, Jim Runyan.

1989

"We have never said we were on a sustained-yield program, and we have never been on a sustained-yield program. Let's get to the heart of it. Sure, its extensively logged, but what is wrong with that?"

> – **Plum Creek**, Rocky Mountain regional operations director, Bill Parson.

FOREWORD

Watching one entire square mile of forest being clearcut, then another, and another in Montana, Idaho, and Washington during the 1980s began for me a painful journey of understanding. Year after year the historic record was methodically pulled together, and the linkages were established between the clearcuts, the log exports, major Northwest timber corporations, and Northwest railroads.

This book chronicles the historic events of the railroad land grant history through the summer of 1994. So alive and dynamic is the land-grant legacy in the Pacific Northwest that the moment this book was finished it was already out of date. Companies enriched by the land grant are on the move. The natural history of the timber industry is to overcut and leave behind stumps and unemployed workers. So it was in New England and so it was in the Great Lakes region. So it is today in the Pacific Northwest, where tensions are escalating over our National Forests.

John Osborn, M.D.

ACKNOWLEDGMENTS

A book of this scope that covers Congress's Northern Pacific land-grant history and the current crisis in American forest policy is not written without talented people and supporting institutions.

The following people critically reviewed the book in part or in its entirety: Matt Andersen, Dennis Baird, Chris Bessler, Janine Blaeloch, Stephen Drinkard, Donald R. Judge (AFL-CIO, Montana), Brock Evans, Mike Green (Department of History, Eastern Washington University), Ross Gorte (Congressional Research Service), Allen Isaacson (former chief hydrologist, Idaho Panhandle National Forests), John Keeble (Department of English, Eastern Washington University), Roxanne Lawler, Harvey Manning, Tom May, Gayle McKellar, Billie Jean Plaster, Mark Solomon, and Carlos Schwantes (Department of History, University of Idaho).

The following foundations provided funding: Blue Mountain Fund, Rockefeller Family Fund, Ruth Mott Fund, and Tides Foundation.

The following people contributed time and talents: Suzanne Daniell and Jim Taft helped craft the scope of this analysis and gave extensively of their time to help in reviewing drafts. Donald Walls created and adapted maps and assisted with the cover. Chuck Carter assisted with layouts, and graphics, and designed the book's cover.

Kate Wilhite helped with computer graphics. Barbara Fulsaas located photographs of the robber barons, timber barons, and presidents. Paul Chesley, James R. Conner, Elizabeth Feryl, Craig Gehrke, Marianne Gordon, Mark Lawler, Ron Reichel, John Rosapepe, Sam Scott, Gerry Snyder and Trygve Steen contributed their photographic talents. Rick Woodbury (Integrated Composition Services) did final scanning and readied photographs for the press. Easy, as production coordinator, choreographed all of the key players and parts and helped us over the last and difficult hurdles in publishing the book.

Finally, *Railroads and Clearcuts* would not exist without the commitment, perseverance, and excellence in scholarship of writer Derrick Jensen and environmental and business historian George Draffan.

John Osborn, M.D.,
    President, Board of Directors,
    Inland Empire Public Lands Council

David Crandall,
    Executive Director,
    Inland Empire Public Lands Council

OVERVIEW

The legacy of the Northern Pacific railroad land grant is alive in the Pacific Northwest and takes the form of log exports, checkerboard forests, unrelenting "public education" campaigns, wealthy lobby groups, and large corporations that wield enormous political and economic influence in the state capitals of the Pacific Northwest and in Washington, D.C.

Because the land-grant forests and land-grant-based timber companies are central to the forest crisis, policymakers will be unable to find adequate solutions for Pacific Northwest forests and communities until they recognize and correct the problems deriving from the 1864 and 1870 land-grant contracts.

The intent of this analysis is to restore to the national debate over forests the central importance of these contracts, the federal laws that are the legal basis for "private" ownership of millions of acres of Pacific Northwest forests, including lands claimed by Plum Creek and the Weyerhaeuser corporate empire (Weyerhaeuser, Potlatch, Boise Cascade).

In 1864, during the Civil War, Congress and President Abraham Lincoln conditionally granted millions of acres of the public domain for the purpose of raising capital to build and maintain a railroad from Lake Superior to the Pacific Ocean. In Section 20 of the law, Congress explicitly retained oversight of the granted lands and may, at any time, "add to, alter, amend, or repeal" the law.

From the beginning, Northern Pacific failed to meet most of the conditions of the 1864 law. Violations of the grant, coupled with serious threats to the public interest, have prompted Congressional oversight of the railroad grant. The most recent major Congressional investigation was requested by President Calvin Coolidge in 1924. The Congressional investigation from 1924-1928 concluded that wrongdoing had occurred. Congress then directed the Department of Justice to take legal action against Northern Pacific in 1929. The partial settlement which followed in 1941 left most of the major issues unresolved.

Figure 1. Pacific Northwest Clearcuts

Checkerboard forests in northeastern Washington State, Colville National Forest. Legacy of Congress's 1864 Northern Pacific railroad land grant.

OVERVIEW OF THE LAND-GRANT ANALYSIS

Railroads and Clearcuts summarizes the railroad history of the 1864 Northern Pacific railroad land grant. Next, it shows how the land-grant forests helped give rise to Plum Creek and the Weyerhaeuser corporate empire (Weyerhaeuser, Potlatch, Boise Cascade). Then, the book analyzes the impacts of overcutting and log exports on Pacific

Northwest forests and communities. Finally, *Railroads and Clearcuts* offers a range of solutions for concerned citizens.

Our analysis is not intended to denigrate railroads, which are recognized as an important part of our nation's transportation infrastructure. Rather, we hope to demonstrate how the 1864 legislation helped create and can also help resolve the current crisis in American forest policy.

History

In 1864 President Lincoln signed into law the largest of the railroad land grants, the Northern Pacific railroad land grant. This law conditionally granted public lands for the purpose of building and maintaining a railroad from Lake Superior to the Pacific Ocean. The law gave public lands for a railroad right-of-way upon which to lay the tracks and 40 million acres (an area slightly smaller than Washington state) to raise capital needed to build and maintain the railroad. The land was granted in alternating square miles, which created a "checkerboard" pattern of ownership that is still visible on maps of many Pacific Northwest forests. The checkerboard pattern was intended to guarantee that railroad access would increase the value of that part of the checkerboard not granted to the railroad.

In 1870, after Congress had extended deadlines, track had still not been built. Financier Jay Cooke persuaded members of Congress to revise the 1864 grant. Congress granted the holders of the grant the right to raise capital by selling bonds, which had not been previously allowed. If Northern Pacific failed financially, then it was to sell the remaining grant lands at local auction. In any case, all lands were to be opened to homesteaders within five years of completing the railroad. In 1873 and again in 1893, Northern Pacific failed financially, but the lands were never legitimately sold at local auction. Ultimately, millions of acres of railroad forests would pass from Northern Pacific to Weyerhaeuser and other corporations.

Land-Grant-Based Timber Corporations

Today Plum Creek, Weyerhaeuser, Potlatch, and Boise Cascade are based on the railroad grant forests which, in turn, are based on the conditions of the 1864 and 1870 contracts.

Plum Creek Timber Company is a direct corporate successor of Northern Pacific. In the 1890s, J.P. Morgan and James J. Hill combined Northern Pacific and Great Northern to form a railroad monopoly across the northern tier states. The Supreme Court struck down the monopoly in 1896 and 1904, but allowed it to stand in 1970. The merger resulted in the formation of Burlington Northern.

In 1980 Burlington Northern segregated itself into a railroad and a holding company for the railroad grant lands. In 1988 this separation became formal and the company divided into a railroad (Burlington Northern Railroad) and a collection of land-grant-based companies (Burlington Resources). Next, Burlington Resources began to "spin off" its subsidiaries. One spin-off from Burlington Resources was Plum Creek Timber Company, which controls the grant forests not previously sold by Northern Pacific/Burlington Northern.

Despite the law requiring that the Northern Pacific grant lands be opened to settlement within five years of completing the railroad, Northern Pacific sold large tracts of the land grant forests to Frederick Weyerhaeuser and his associates. Weyerhaeuser purchased millions of acres of land-grant forests in the Great Lakes region and the Pacific Northwest, mostly during the 1890s and early 1900s. The largest of the many Weyerhaeuser purchases was 900,000 acres in Washington state in 1899. Weyerhaeuser subsequently incorporated Potlatch and Boise Payette (later Boise Cascade) to cut lands obtained in Idaho.

The largest purchase of Northern Pacific grant lands in Montana was about a million acres bought by Amalgamated Copper Company (later Anaconda) in 1907. About 670,000 acres of these land-grant forests were purchased by Champion International in 1972. Champion began liquidating the land-grant forests in the 1970s, and in 1993 sold these lands to Plum Creek.

OVERCUTTING

In 1864 the Pacific Northwest's forests had not yet been logged and extended from the continental divide across parts of the Columbia River Watershed to the Pacific Ocean. Across this same region today, watersheds are unraveling and the spotted owl, the marbled murrelet, the grizzly bear, many runs of salmon, and other species of flora and fauna have become threatened, endangered or extinct through the last century of excessive logging.

The checkerboard pattern of the railroad forests complicates management of the National Forests. Management philosophies alternate by the square mile, precluding efforts to manage forests as ecosystems. Cumulative environmental damage from overcutting the railroad checkerboard forests has constrained logging activities in adjoining National Forests.

LOG EXPORTS

Many of the raw wood materials exported to Japan and other Pacific Rim nations originate from lands conditionally granted to build a railroad. These land-grant logs, cants, and wood chips bypass local mills and opportunities for value-added industries. Because of loopholes in federal log export reform legislation passed in 1990, companies such as Plum Creek can export land-grant logs to lucrative foreign markets, convert foreign profits to American dollars, and then use those dollars to bid against smaller domestic mills for an increasingly scarce timber supply available from the National Forests of the Pacific Northwest.

OPTIONS TO INTERVENE

Oversight authority of the railroad grant lands is explicitly provided to Congress in Section 20 of the 1864 grant. Congress has exerted oversight several times since 1864. Failure to fulfill contractual obligations has led Congress to take back millions of acres of railroad grant lands and restore them to public ownership. Major revestments (or forfeitures) occurred in 1890, involving Northern Pacific and other railroad companies, and in 1916 when Congress revested the Oregon & California railroad grant lands in western Oregon.

In 1924 President Calvin Coolidge asked Congress to investigate the Northern Pacific grant. Coolidge noted in his letter to Congress that the defaults by Northern Pacific on the "contract or covenant" were "numerous and flagrant." The Congressional investigation which followed prompted the Attorney General to recommend judicial review of the grant. Congress voted to seek court action against Northern Pacific. Despite a partial settlement in 1941, major legal issues raised by President Coolidge and Congress were never resolved and have not been resolved to this day.

The full extent of the public trust obligations pertaining to the 1864 and 1870 laws has yet to be defined by Congress and by the courts. These efforts at clarification could start by revisiting the work begun with the 1924 Coolidge investigation and the subsequent court case.

After completing a thorough investigation, Congress could restore land-grant forests to the public. Such action would be especially important in correcting the checkerboard land ownership pattern that precludes sound, ecosystem-based management in National Forests. Restoring land-grant forests to the public could be accomplished through purchase, exchange, or revestment.

Congress could address the problem of exporting land-grant logs by amending either the 1990 reform legislation or the 1864 and 1870 land-grant law to prohibit the export of unprocessed logs and fiber from grant lands.

The crisis for Pacific Northwest forests and communities has at its core the 1864 Northern Pacific railroad land grant, the defining piece of legislation for the Pacific Northwest. Understanding railroad land-grant history opens the door to solutions for resolving the forest crisis. Congress may amend legislation, a power granted to it in the United States Constitution. In the specific case of the 1864 Northern Pacific land grant, Section 20 explicitly provides Congress with oversight of the land grant. Section 20 states:

> . . . Congress may, at any time, having due regard for the rights of said Northern Pacific Railroad Company, add to, alter, amend, or repeal this act.

HISTORY

CONGRESS'S NORTHERN PACIFIC LAND GRANTS

In 1864, during the Civil War, the United States Congress created the Northern Pacific Railroad Company and empowered it to construct a rail line from Lake Superior to Puget Sound.[1] To aid in the construction and maintenance of the railroad, Congress conditionally granted Northern Pacific nearly 40 million acres of land.[2] Forty million acres equals more than 2 percent of the land mass of the 48 contiguous United States and more land than this nation's nine smallest states put together.

---

[1] 13 Stat. 366. The first number refers to the federal statutes' volume number, and the last number refers to the page within the volume. The statute is reprinted in Appendix 1.

[2] Northern Pacific eventually claimed 38.6 million acres, or 61,875 square miles. Mergers brought the total claimed by Northern Pacific's corporate successors to 48 million acres. This includes the 1850 Chicago, Burlington & Quincy grant at 2.8 million acres, the 1862 St. Paul & Pacific grant at 3.3 million (from the state of Minnesota), the 1864 Northern Pacific grant at 38.6 million, and the 1879 St. Paul, Minneapolis & Manitoba grant of 2.6 million acres. The two St. Paul grants were later controlled by Great Northern, which in 1970 merged with Burlington Northern, the corporate heir of Northern Pacific and current holder of the 1864 grant (for land-grant acreages, see Root, 1987, p.120; Wilner, 1981, pp.698-699; and Gates, 1968, p. 362).

Not all of this land was patented to the companies. For example, Northern Pacific was forced by Congress to forfeit two million acres of grant land in 1890 (26 Stat. 496). An exhaustive review of acreages granted, claimed, patented, and revested is beyond the scope of this book.

The grant contained numerous conditions, including: starting date for construction, types of land Northern Pacific was allowed to claim, and completion date. In addition, Congress reserved for itself the right, with due respect for the rights of Northern Pacific, to "add to, alter, amend, or repeal this act."[3]

The granted land fell into two categories, defined by their utility to the railroad. The first category, by far the smallest portion of the land grant, consisted of ground for the tracks and a two hundred-foot right-of-way to each side, as well as land for stations, workshops, depots, etc.

The vast majority of the land was a subsidy to aid in the construction and maintenance of the railroad.[4] In essence, the railroad was to be given every other square mile (section) of land in a band 40 miles wide through states (Wisconsin, Minnesota, and Oregon) and 80 miles wide through territories (North Dakota, Montana, Idaho, and Washington) from Lake Superior to the Pacific Ocean, with a branch to Portland.[5] Northern Pacific was not to receive land for the branch to Portland.[6] Since the land was granted in alternating square miles, a "checkerboard" pattern of ownership was created that is still visible on maps and landscapes of many Pacific Northwest forests.

Northern Pacific was not allowed to claim lands which had already been occupied by settlers.[7] In lieu of previously claimed lands, Northern Pacific was allowed to choose property in a strip between 40 and 50 miles from the tracks. These additional bands became commonly known as "in lieu lands" or "indemnity strips."

Nor was Northern Pacific allowed to claim lands which contained minerals other than coal or iron.[8] In exchange, the company was once

---

[3]   13 Stat. 366-372. The authority of Congress to legislate is granted by the Constitution in any case.

[4]   13 Stat. 367 and 372.

[5]   The lands were granted in a checkerboard fashion on the assumption that the increased access provided by the railroad would raise the value of the government's share of the checkerboards.

[6]   These lands were added in the 1870 grant to the Northern Pacific Company (16 Stat. 378; and Schwinden, 1950, p.51) and were the lands forfeited back to the government in 1890.

[7]   13 Stat. 368.

[8]   Railroad use of coal has been restricted by a complex set of laws and court rulings.

again allowed to extend the band within which it could claim lands, which increased the width of the giant checkerboard.[9]

Northern Pacific failed to meet the conditions of the grant even before laying the first mile of track. Congress had specified that failure to sell two million dollars worth of stock to the public within two years of the 1864 act would void the grant.[10] Northern Pacific failed to do so.[11] Further, Congress specified that work was to begin within two years. However, Northern Pacific did not begin construction for six years.[12]

In 1870 Northern Pacific approached Congress for permission to sell bonds mortgaging the as-yet-unowned grant lands.[13] Northern Pacific was assisted in this request by the largest banking house in the nation, that of Jay Cooke and Company. Jay Cooke used his money to "gain the votes of recalcitrant Congressmen."[14] "Loans" and stock were given liberally, not only to Congressmen, but to Vice-President Schuyler Colfax and to editors of influential newspapers, including Horace Greeley of the *New York Tribune*.[15] Many of the most prominent and vocal supporters of the railroad, such as future President Rutherford B. Hayes, Secretary of the Treasury Hugh McCulloch, and preacher Henry Ward Beecher, also held financial interest in the company.[16] In fact, Northern Pacific was a corporation that included politicians, businessmen, and other influential figures of the day, including, for example, Ulysses S. Grant and John C. Fremont.[17]

Northern Pacific's opponents included not only backers of other land-grant railroads but also those who represented growing public

---

[9]   13 Stat. 368.

[10]   13 Stat. 372.

[11]   Smalley, 1883, pp.124,129; and 311 U.S. 335. For an extensive contemporary history of Northern Pacific between 1864 and 1883, written by a consultant working for Northern Pacific, see Smalley's *History of the Northern Pacific Railroad.*

[12]   Smalley, 1883, p.185.

[13]   Smalley, 1883, p.137ff.

[14]   Schwinden, 1950, p.56, citing Oberholtzer, 1907, pp.175-176.

[15]   Horace Greeley gave the famous advice, "Go West, young man."

[16]   Sobel, 1988, pp.167-168.

[17]   The list of incorporators is given in 13 Stat. 366. The statute is printed in Appendix 1.

resentment of the railroad land-grant policies.[18] The opponents argued that in the original grant Northern Pacific had at its own request been given twice as much land per mile as other railroad companies in exchange for not issuing bonds.[19] To allow Northern Pacific to now issue bonds would defeat the purpose of the original grant's size.

Northern Pacific – and Jay Cooke's money – prevailed, and Congress allowed Northern Pacific to issue bonds on the grant lands.[20] It also granted lands for the previously excluded spur to Portland and increased the size of both indemnity strips by ten to 20 miles. Northern Pacific's path of potential ownership thus was enlarged to 120 miles in the territories.[21]

Restrictive clauses were incorporated into the 1870 legislation:

> All lands hereby granted to said company which shall not be sold or disposed of or remain subject to the mortgage by this act authorized, at the expiration of five years after the completion of the entire road, shall be subject to settlement and preemption like other lands, at a price to be paid to said company not exceeding two dollars and fifty cents per acre; and if the mortgage hereby authorized shall at any time be enforced by foreclosure or other legal proceeding, or the mortgaged lands hereby granted or any of them, be sold by the trustees to whom such mortgage may be executed, whether at its maturity or for any failure or default of said company under the terms thereof, such lands shall be sold at public sale . . . in single sections or subdivisions thereof, to the highest and best bidder. . . . [22]

The maximum price, size of parcel, and even whether all grant lands were to be sold have been the subject of controversy ever since. Congress's intent and the Court's interpretations are still disputed.

---

18   Smalley, 1883, p.138.
19   Smalley, 1883, p.114.
20   16 Stat. 378. The statute is printed in Appendix 2.
21   16 Stat. 378.
22   16 Stat. 378.

NORTHERN PACIFIC HOLDS TIGHT TO THE LAND GRANT THROUGH BANKRUPTCY AND CONSTRUCTION

In 1870 Jay Cooke began an intense public relations campaign to sell Northern Pacific bonds. Knowing (according to Jay Cooke's New York partner, Harris Fahnestock) that the bonds were being sold "almost exclusively to persons who rely upon our recommendations rather than upon their own judgments,"[23] Jay Cooke hired a writer to create a vision of the grant lands which could easily be sold.

The writer, Sam Wilkerson, began to write of "a vast wilderness waiting like a rich heiress to be appropriated and enjoyed."[24] The physical description was similarly exuberant, equating, in a typical example, the climate of Montana to "the mildness of Southern Ohio."[25]

Newspapers failing to write favorable editorials were threatened with loss of advertising revenue and the editors were threatened with the loss of their jobs.[26]

In 1870 and 1871 the bonds brought in nearly $30 million, much of which came from the "small savings of thousands of mechanics, farmers, and tradesmen."[27]

Northern Pacific promptly bought out the St. Paul and Pacific Railroad; when Northern Pacific later failed, so did the St. Paul and Pacific.[28] They also bought controlling interest in an Oregon steamboat line.[29]

Even though Cooke knew, according to Fahnestock, that Northern Pacific's management was "inefficient, distracted by other engagements and extravagant to the last degree," Cooke continued to assure the public of the "intelligence, vigor and economy of [Northern Pacific's] management."[30]

---

[23] June 1872 letter from Fahnestock to Cooke, quoted in Minnegerode, 1927, p.71.

[24] Quoted in Sobel, 1988, p.167.

[25] Smalley, 1883, p.174.

[26] See, for example, O'Connor, 1953, p.95, and Winks, 1991, p.191.

[27] Smalley, 1883, p.172.

[28] Hidy, Hidy, and Scott, 1988, pp.21-24.

[29] Smalley, 1883, pp.187-188. The line was the Oregon Steam Navigation Company.

[30] Minnegerode, 1927, p.71.

The sales of the bonds began to fade, however, and through 1872 sales were unable to keep up with Northern Pacific's prolific spending. To keep the appearance of a strong market for Northern Pacific's bonds, Cooke took to quietly buying back $90,000 of every $100,000 worth of bonds he would sell.[31]

This worked only for a while, and when Northern Pacific fell, so did Jay Cooke and Company. Unable to meet their debts, Jay Cooke and Company's New York offices were forced to close on September 18, 1873. His Philadelphia offices failed immediately thereafter, as did his First National Bank of Washington.[32]

Northern Pacific's overextension was representative of the overextension of the economy of the entire nation. Banks fell like dominos. Thirty banks in New York and Philadelphia failed on September 19.[33] On the 20th, President Grant closed the New York Stock Exchange for ten days.[34] The federal debt, which had previously been decreasing by $1 million per day, began to shoot back up.[35]

Jay Cooke and Company's failure precipitated the nation's worst depression to that time. Over the next five years, business declined 32 percent.[36] The number of business failures nationwide climbed from 2,915 in 1871 to 5,183 in 1873, and to 10,478 in 1879.[37] Hundreds of thousands of workers were forced out of their jobs.[38]

In 1875, in the aftermath of the collapse, Northern Pacific reorganized. Frederick Billings, who later became president of Northern Pacific, created a reorganization plan in which the existing mortgage would be foreclosed, and stock would be substituted for the outstanding bonds. The assets, including the grant, were to be bought by a committee of interested bondholders. Despite the possible violation of the Congressional intent that the land be auctioned publicly after foreclosure, and despite the complaints of dissident bondholders, the bankruptcy judge in charge of the case accepted the settlement.[39]

---

[31]   Smalley, 1883, p.196.
[32]   Sobel, 1988, p.179.
[33]   Smalley, 1883, p.199.
[34]   Minnegerode, 1927, p.77.
[35]   Smalley, 1883, p.199.
[36]   Sobel, 1988, p.192.
[37]   U.S. Bureau of the Census, 1973, p.913.
[38]   Smalley, 1883, p.199.
[39]   Smalley, 1883, pp.206-210; and Applegate, 1979, p.15.

Following reorganization, Northern Pacific continued construction of the railroad line. In 1883, four years after its twice-extended deadline for completion had passed, the company completed its main line. The final spike was driven at Gold Creek, Montana, on September 8, 1883.[40]

CREATING A RAILROAD MONOPOLY

The next ten years were not kind to the Northern Pacific. It was "poorly built," and "costing half again as much to operate as the Great Northern (Northern Pacific's main competitor), the Northern Pacific was hopelessly handicapped in the race for traffic. The panic of 1893 caused it to fail again, hence sweeping it again into receivership."[41]

The 1893 financial collapse of Northern Pacific created trouble both for J.P. Morgan, who controlled the Northern Pacific, and for James J. Hill, owner of the Great Northern. Morgan feared for the loss of the granted lands, and Hill feared that Northern Pacific, in bankruptcy, might cut its rates when freed of its obligation to pay interest.[42]

Their solution was to combine the two lines. Morgan and Hill succeeded in doing this, creating a monopoly across the northern states,[43] and once again avoiding the loss of the granted lands. Morgan was to head the trustees in whom the voting power of the stockholders was vested,[44] and Hill, with a reputation for being a solid and thrifty railroad man, would run both railroads.[45]

In 1896 the United States Supreme Court held this consolidation of parallel and competing railroad corporations to be an illegal restraint of trade.[46] Hill's response was to set up joint ownership of the

---

[40]   Glaspell, 1941, p.187.
[41]   Winkler, 1950, p.165. After this second failure, the lands were sold at public sale to the highest bidder, as required by the 1870 resolution (16 Stat. 378). But, "the new [Northern Pacific] railway company was reported in every instance the highest bidder" (Heath v. Northern Pacific, 38 L.D. 770, 1909).
[42]   Martin, 1976, pp.440-441.
[43]   Pyle, 1968, pp.14-16; originally published in 1916-1917.
[44]   Pyle, 1968, p.25.
[45]   Jackson, 1983, p.181.
[46]   161 U.S. 646 (1896). Morgan was, of course, in control of many other railroads as well. The "morganization" of railroads and the resulting investigations by, among others, Louis Brandeis, Woodrow Wilson, and Harry Truman are traced by Chernow, 1990.

two rail lines by individuals instead of by a corporation. This effectively sidestepped the Supreme Court ruling.[47]

In 1896 Morgan refinanced Northern Pacific with 100- and 150-year bonds, using several million acres of grant lands as collateral. This made the railroad once again solvent, and effectively bound a portion of the granted lands to the railroad.[48]

In 1901 Hill and his backers bought controlling interest in another railroad: the Chicago, Burlington & Quincy, a line whose access to Chicago was also coveted by E.H. Harriman of the Union Pacific. Harriman attempted a hostile takeover of Northern Pacific through secret stock purchases. Northern Pacific's stock price surged. But Harriman's efforts fell short, and the stock price collapsed, taking much of Wall Street down with them.[49] The *New York Times* reported, "It was more than a panic; it was a wholesale sacrifice of prices and of people – a sacrifice, it is generally agreed, if not to the greed, at least to the stupidity and vaulting ambition of men, leaders in the financial and railroad world, who in their efforts to secure control of a great railroad property sacrificed all things else."[50]

A reporter asked J.P. Morgan, "Don't you think that since you are being blamed for a panic that has ruined thousands of people and disturbed a whole nation, some statement is due to the public?"

Despite the fact that Northern Pacific's wealth was derived from Congress, and ultimately from the public domain, Morgan responded, "I owe the public nothing."[51]

In the aftermath of Harriman's failed takeover attempt, Hill and Morgan created a holding company for the three railroads, believing

---

[47] Pyle, 1968, p.24.

[48] Because of these bonds, Northern Pacific and its heirs were unable to separate rights to 2.4 million acres of the grant lands, with the surface and mineral rights to an additional 1.9 million acres of grant lands, from the railroad until a much later date than were the other land grant railroads. The bonds were settled in 1988, enabling the separation of Burlington Resources from Burlington Northern Railroad, (Miller, 1987; and Rievman v. Burlington Northern, 118 F.R.D. 29, S.D.N.Y., 1987).

[49] J.P. Morgan's financial firm managed to profit from the panic, joining a pool which made call money available to harried stockbrokers at up to 60 percent interest (Sinclair, 1981, p.135).

[50] *New York Times*, May 10, 1901.

[51] Jackson, 1983, p.213.

the holding company would simply be too large for anyone to take over. It was called Northern Securities Company.[52]

In 1904 the United States Supreme Court again ruled that the competing lines could not merge; the Northern Securities Company violated the Sherman Anti-Trust Act.[53]

The formal separation of the companies was accomplished merely by giving the stockholders of each railroad equal shares of the other company. As Hill said, "Two certificates of stock are now issued instead of one. They are printed in different colors. That is the main difference."[54] He also said, "I have not yet read the complete decision, but I wish to say that the three roads are still there, and there they will remain, despite the learned jurists of the Supreme Court of the United States. The properties are as good as ever, and they will continue to make money for their stockholders."[55]

After the 1920 Transportation Act exempted railroads from the Sherman Anti-Trust Act, the three railroads tried to merge again. In 1922, 61 percent of the Northern Pacific and Great Northern stock was held by the same shareholders. Then, in 1930, the Interstate Commerce Commission (ICC) approved a merger with the proviso that the Chicago, Burlington & Quincy be divested, but the merger was dropped because the Chicago, Burlington & Quincy was the biggest money-maker of the three.[56]

Throughout its history, the management of Northern Pacific has continually circumvented the law and maintained the practical merger that began in 1895 and that would eventually become Burlington Northern Railroad.

CALVIN COOLIDGE AND THE **1924 - 1928** CONGRESSIONAL INVESTIGATION

In 1906 Northern Pacific began to survey an additional three million acres the company believed due it under the 1864 grant. However, these particular lands had since been withdrawn as National

---

[52]   Sinclair, 1981, p.136.
[53]   Northern Securities Co. v. United States, 193 U.S. 197 (1904).
[54]   Holbrook, 1955, p.144.
[55]   Yenne, 1991, p.74.
[56]   Bechtold, 1991.

Forests. This threat to the nation's conservation policies prompted President Calvin Coolidge in 1924 to ask Congress to undertake a thorough review of the Northern Pacific grant.[57]

In April of 1924, Congress authorized its investigation of the 1864 and 1870 grants, still the most thorough investigation of Northern Pacific's grants to date.[58] The hearings lasted five years and involved dozens of witnesses. Among other things, the hearings found that while railroad construction had cost Northern Pacific $70 million, land sales alone had brought the company $136 million. Even by the 1920s, the land grant was worth at least four times the cost of construction, not including the value of the coal.[59] Further, allegations arising from the hearings formed the basis of a lawsuit by the government to adjust the grant and to settle the legal questions which had surrounded the grant since its inception.[60] Some of the government's allegations included the following:[61]

- Northern Pacific had not sold stock to the public, as had been required by Congress (311 U.S. 335);[62]

- Northern Pacific had not built the railroad according to the Congressionally mandated schedule (311 U.S. 336);

---

[57]   See the statement by Calvin Coolidge (in Appendix 3 reprinted from the *New York Times*, Feb. 26, 1924); see also Applegate, 1979, pp.30-33. A description of the legal actions by Northern Pacific and the government in the 18 years between the initial threat and government's response is beyond the scope of this book. For a description of these actions, see Cotroneo, 1980, p.109ff; and "The Forest Reserve Case," U.S. v. Northern Pacific, 256 U.S. 51 (1921).

[58]   U.S. Congress, 1924-1928.

[59]   The figures of $70 million construction cost and $136 million in gross receipts by mid-1917 are from a letter from U.S. Department of Agriculture Secretary Wallace to President Coolidge, Feb. 19, 1924 (*New York Times*, Feb. 26, 1924). A figure from the Congressional hearings of the 1920s shows net grant land receipts of $100 million by 1927 (Mercer, 1982, p.200). For land sales after 1922, see *Moody's Transportation Manual* (1970, p.722). Mercer (1982) and Henry (1945) discuss the value of the land grants at length.

[60]   This was the case that was decided in U.S. v. Northern Pacific, 311 U.S. 317 (1940) and settled in U.S. v. Northern Pacific, 41 F.Supp. 273 (1941).

[61]   The following are not the only examples of fraud with which Northern Pacific has been charged. A comprehensive listing would quickly become a book of its own. A few examples should suffice to give the flavor. In 1871 Northern

- Northern Pacific did not open its lands to settlement and preemption as required by Congressional mandate (311 U.S. 337);

- more than a million acres had been fraudulently classified as mineral lands, so that Northern Pacific could claim prime agricultural or timber land in lieu (355 U.S. 355 and 358);

- 1.4 million acres too many had been claimed and granted in Washington state (311 U.S. 349);

- Northern Pacific wrongfully received 13.3 million acres located within Native American reservations (311 U.S. 347);

- Northern Pacific had illegally diverted funds to the building of branch lines (311 U.S. 336); and

---

Pacific and the federal government joined forces to fight the illegal cutting of trees on federal lands. The United States attorney L. Holmes assigned a deputy to Northern Pacific attorney Hazard Stevens, the son of the Washington Territorial Governor, and gave Northern Pacific blank subpoenas to issue to poachers. Eventually Stevens used this authority to profit from the illegal cutting of federal timber: for a deposit of $100 and a rate of 50 cents per thousand board feet, a person could cut federal timber without interference from Stevens. The U.S. General Land Office finally intervened in June 1873 and accused Stevens of stealing from the government and the railroad. Stevens was not charged, but Northern Pacific fired him (Ficken, 1987, pp.40,44-47). Northern Pacific was eventually indicted for stealing timber (see also Steen, 1969, pp.46-47). In the 1880s, the Northwestern Improvement Company, a Northern Pacific subsidiary, was also indicted for theft of public timber in Washington; it had logged far from its railroad right-of-way and had even set up sawmills on public land. It faced federal suits for several hundred thousand dollars, but witnesses were hard to find because local people usually favored local industry (Steen, 1969, pp.46-47, citing U.S. Dept. of Interior Reports from 1885 and 1886). Northern Pacific itself was indicted in Olympia, Washington, for collecting stumpage in advance for timber cut from "its" land (Steen, 1969, p.47, citing Fairweather, 1919, pp. 96-99).

[62] The citation numbers for these charges are from the 1940 United States Supreme Court decision in U.S. v. Northern Pacific, 311 U.S. 317. The government's charges in this case stemmed from the 1924-1928 Congressional hearings.

- Northern Pacific had delayed surveying vast portions of the land grant in order to avoid paying taxes (311 U.S. 317).

At the request of Congress, the Attorney General reviewed the issues and advised that Congress could declare part or all of the land grant forfeited and that Congress should submit the entire dispute to the courts.[63] In 1929 Congress voted, with President Hoover's approval, to authorize the Department of Justice to bring suit against Northern Pacific:

- to return a million and a half acres to the public domain based on Northern Pacific's use of an unnecessarily circuitous route through Washington;

- to clear governmental claim to 2.4 million acres of land already returned to the public domain based on alleged erroneous classification as mineral lands by Northern Pacific; and

- for a general accounting and clarification of the issues pertaining to the grant.[64]

In 1930 the U.S. Attorney General filed suit in Spokane, Washington.[65] The convoluted legal maneuvering during the next ten years is beyond the scope of *Railroads and Clearcuts*. However, in 1940 the case went before the U.S. Supreme Court. Only eight justices gave opinions, the ninth having disqualified himself for previous involvement in the land-grant investigation.[66] While expressly reserving judgement for later consideration, these eight justices disagreed on the following points:

---

[63]   U.S. Congress, 1924-1928.

[64]   46 Stat. 41, 42, and 43; *New York Times*, June 26, 1929; *Spokane Chronicle*, Aug. 1, 1930; *Spokesman-Review*, Aug. 1, 1930; *New York Times*, Aug. 1, 1930; Applegate, pp.36-37; and 46 Stat. 41, section 5.

[65]   311 U.S. 317 (1940).

[66]   311 U.S. 376 (1940).

- whether Northern Pacific had legitimately sold stock to the public in the first two years after its charter (if not, then the grant was null and void) (311 U.S. 335);

- whether Northern Pacific had finished construction as required (311 U.S. 336);

- whether funds had been channeled to branches while the main line went unfinished (311 U.S. 336);

- whether lands had been opened to settlement and preemption at $2.50 an acre (311 U.S. 337); and

- whether the grant had been violated by Northern Pacific's actions following the 1875 and 1896 foreclosures (311 U.S. 340).

The rest of the decision generally favored the United States, and the case was remanded to a lower court so the U.S. could present evidence for fraud.[67]

In 1941 Northern Pacific proposed a settlement. In effect, if the government would consent to close the fraud case against the Northern Pacific, then the railroad would relinquish claims to 2.9 million acres and agree to pay the U.S. $300,000.[68] The Secretaries of the Interior and of Agriculture agreed, as did the land committees of Congress, and the settlement was approved, despite reservations by the presiding judge: "Congress has not authorized the settlement. The act which was taken by the Committees is not an act of Congress, and is in no way binding on the Congress."[69]

Despite the judge's statements; despite the fact that Congress explicitly retained to itself the right to, at any time, "add to, alter, amend, or repeal this act"; and despite the fact that even without this statement Congress retains the Constitutional authority to add to, alter, amend, or repeal any act, there are those who assert that the

---

[67]   U.S. v. Northern Pacific, 311 U.S. 317, 342. The subsequent judgement was never made.

[68]   U.S. v. Northern Pacific, 41 F. Supp. 273 (1941); and Cotroneo, 1980.

[69]   U.S. v. Northern Pacific, 41 F. Supp. 287 to 291 (1941).

settlement of 1941 closed the land-grant question.[70] In 1981 the Congressional Research Service investigated the legal history of the land grant and concluded that Congress continues to retain the authority to resolve issues pertaining to the 1864 and 1870 grants.[71] Or, as restated by the president of the Water Transportation Association, John Creedy, in 1983, "Congress gave the land grant, Congress specified the obligations, Congress can resolve any issues involving what obligations remain, and Congress can decide what statutory changes are needed to provide appropriate protection of the public interest."[72]

Since 1941 Congress has sporadically attempted to address some of the remaining issues of the land grant. For example, in 1982, stating

---

[70]   These include Cotroneo, 1980; Wilner, 1981; and Bressler, the chairman of Burlington Northern, in Creedy, 1983, p.157. Cotroneo is a historian who has had singular access to Northern Pacific corporate records. Wilner was an employee of the Association of American Railroads. Burlington Northern is the corporate descendant of Northern Pacific.

There is also a widespread impression (see, for example, Long, May 23, 1993) that the 1983 court case Citizens' Committee to Save the Land Grant Railroads v. Burlington Northern ruled that there were "no limitations on the power of [Burlington Northern] to dispose of the lands." But the 1983 case against Burlington Northern's formation of a holding company that would lead to spin-offs was dismissed by the court on narrow grounds. Judge Betty B. Fletcher of the 9th Circuit Court of Appeals said the "transfer of assets of railroad corporation to holding company and its nonrailroad subsidiaries did not violate the Northern Pacific Land Grant Act of *1864*. . . . An alleged violation of the bond indentures could conceivably be within the court's federal jurisdiction. . . . However, since plaintiffs do not argue that the question whether Burlington has breached the terms of the bond indentures somehow depends on the interpretation of the provisions of the Act or any other federal law, plaintiffs bond related claim is not a federal question. . . . [E]ven if a private cause of action may lie against the railroad for violations of the terms of the Act, no violations of the Act were alleged here and the bond-related claim presents no federal questions." (Citizens' Committee to Save the Land Grant Railroads v. Burlington Northern, 708 F.2d 1430 (June 22, 1983)) [emphasis added]. In other words, the plaintiffs sued, and the court dismissed, on narrow grounds of jurisdiction rather than of substance. The 1983 case was never intended to be a final settlement. The court made a clear effort to rule only on the grounds which were presented to it and left other troubling issues unresolved.

[71]   Baldwin, 1981.

[72]   Creedy, 1983, p.156.

that "Congress must decide whether the public still has a right to demand service from the railroads as a result of the enormous grants of land they received," Representative Pat Williams (D-MT) called for hearings on the land grants.[73] During a special hearing of the Senate Judiciary Committee on "Rail Mergers and the Formation of the BN Holding Company," Senator Max Baucus (D-MT) had the following exchange with Burlington Northern's Chairman Richard Bressler:

> **Senator Baucus**: Is it BN's position that there are no continuing obligations of any kind arising out of the Northern Pacific land grants?
> **Mr. Bressler**: Continuing obligations?
> **Senator Baucus**: Yes.
> **Mr. Bressler**: No, we do not recognize any continuing obligations.[74]

In 1901 J. P. Morgan said, "I owe the public nothing." In 1982 his corporate heir Richard Bressler said, "No, we do not recognize any continuing obligations."

While Congress passed and Abraham Lincoln signed the 1864 Northern Pacific railroad land grant to promote the public interest, and while Congress explicitly reserved to itself oversight authority, the railroad company and its corporate heirs deny that public interest. As we will show, this lack of Congressional oversight has resulted in the overcutting of the forests of the Pacific Northwest, the squeezing out of small mills with consequent collapse of rural economies, and the exportation of raw logs from granted lands, all by Congress's land-grant-based national and multinational timber corporations.

---

[73] Andrews, 1982.
[74] Creedy, 1983, p.157.

UNHITCHING THE LAND GRANT FROM THE RAILROADS, 1967 TO 1992

In 1967 the U.S. Interstate Commerce Commission approved the merger of Northern Pacific, Great Northern, and Chicago, Burlington & Quincy. Thus was formed Burlington Northern, corporate heir to three land-grant railroad empires.[75]

With both the public and Congress quiet on the grant lands, the only question facing Burlington Northern as a corporation beholden to its shareholders was how to maximize profit from the lands it controlled.

A major obstacle in the managers' way was the lien on the bonds sold by J.P. Morgan in 1896. The bonds prevented Northern Pacific, and later Burlington Northern, from separating many of the lands from the railroad.[76]

In 1987, after a protracted court fight, Burlington Northern was able to break the lien which bound portions of the grant lands to the bonds by paying the bondholders $35.5 million. The settlement released for Burlington Northern's use 2.4 million acres of land and surface and mineral rights to an additional 1.9 million acres.[77]

These are not the only lands held by the corporate descendants of the Northern Pacific empire. In 1988 Burlington Northern held the mineral rights to 8.5 million acres.[78] It held 16.3 billion tons of coal and 3.5 million ounces of gold.[79] It held 4.6 trillion cubic feet of

---

[75]   331 ICC 228. Upheld by the United States Supreme Court in 1970 (U.S. v. ICC, 396 U.S. 491).

Great Northern is often said to be the only non-grant transcontinental railroad, but Great Northern *was* the beneficiary of two land grants totalling 5.6 million acres (Mercer, 1982, p.56; Root, 1987; and Gates, 1968, p. 362).

[76]   Miller, 1987; and Burlington Northern merger documents filed with the ICC.

[77]   Rievman v. Burlington Northern, 118 F.R.D. 29, S.D.N.Y., 1987. Note the inclusion of mineral rights despite the clear mandate of Congress that Northern Pacific not receive lands bearing minerals other than iron or coal.

[78]   Under its Meridian Minerals subsidiary (Burlington Resources, June 2, 1988). By 1991 Burlington Resources held mineral rights to 13.3 million acres (*Bloomberg Business News*, March 2, 1993).

[79]   Again, by Meridian (Burlington Resources, 1991 Annual Report, p.15; Burlington Resources, July 7, 1988; and *Seattle Post-Intelligencer,* Nov. 30,

natural gas, enough to supply half the natural gas burned in California.[80] It held nearly a million acres of commercial and industrial property along 25,000 miles of track in 23 states.[81] It controlled 10.5 billion board feet of old-growth timber on 1.5 million acres.[82]

Since 1988 the story of Burlington Northern has been that of unhitching this vast wealth from the railroad. It has done this by creating Burlington Resources, a corporation which held the assets of the grant lands without being encumbered with the debts of Burlington Northern Railroad. Burlington Northern CEO Gerald Grinstein was quoted in *Forbes* magazine as saying, "The standing joke was that they [Burlington Resources] got the gold and we got the shaft."[83] In 1989 Burlington Resources spun off Plum Creek Timber Company, with its 1.5 million acres of grant lands.[84] Plum Creek represents only about 4 percent of the assets of the land-grant companies.[85]

Since then, Burlington Resources has created numerous other companies through spin-offs and other transactions. These companies include: El Paso Natural Gas;[86] Great Northern Properties, the largest private owner of coal in the United States;[87] Meridian Oil and several royalty companies, the largest independent holder of gas and oil

---

1988). Note, once again, the inclusion of a gold mining company despite clear Congressional intent that the granted lands not include mineral lands.

[80] Through one of its subsidiaries, El Paso Natural Gas (Burlington Resources, June 2, 1988, p.28).

[81] The land was held through its subsidiary Glacier Park (Burlington Resources, June 2, 1988, pp.41-42).

[82] Through Plum Creek Timber (Burlington Resources, 1988, p.36). In 1991, Plum Creek accounted for only 3.7 percent of the assets and 5.2 percent of the sales and profits of the combined corporate empire (calculated from financial data in the 1991 Annual Reports for Burlington Northern, Burlington Resources, and Plum Creek).

[83] Norman, March 30, 1992, p.46.

[84] Plum Creek, May 1989. Plum Creek's holdings in late 1993 had increased to 2.1 million acres (Dow Jones, Nov. 2, 1993).

[85] Calculated from the total assets shown in the 1992 Annual Reports of Burlington Northern (p.27), Burlington Resources (p.15), and Plum Creek (p.16); and El Paso Natural Gas, March 12, 1992 *Prospectus*, (p.F4).

[86] El Paso, March 22, 1992.

[87] Dow Jones, Oct. 28, 1992.

reserves in the United States;[88] Meridian Gold (which merged with FMC Corporation in 1991); and many others. The assets of Burlington Northern, Burlington Resources, El Paso Natural Gas, and Plum Creek alone were worth more than $15.5 billion in 1991.[89] The various spin-offs had raised $1.4 billion by early 1993, according to Burlington Resources CEO Thomas O'Leary.[90]

In making the 1864 land grant, Congress hoped to "promote the public interest and welfare by the construction of said railroad . . . and keeping the same in working order, and to secure to the government at all times . . . the use and benefits of same for postal, military, and other purposes."[91]

Some members of Congress feared that it would also create a vast empire for the railroad. Part of today's "unintended empire"[92] and "perpetual monopoly"[93] consists of enormous public forests which were transferred from the public domain to the holdings of giant timber companies. *Railroads and Clearcuts* focuses on these railroad-based timber companies and their impacts on the forests and communities of the Pacific Northwest.[94]

---

[88]   Burlington Resources 1990 Annual Report, p. 1; *Seattle Post-Intelligencer*, June 14, 1993.

[89]   These figures are calculated from their 1991 and 1992 Annual Reports. This wealth is further described in Burlington Resources, June 2, 1988; and *Marple's Business Newsletter*, 1988.

[90]   Virgin, March 20, 1993.

[91]   13 Stat. 372.

[92]   As it was called by Applegate, 1979.

[93]   By Senator Howell in the Senate debates of April 20, 1870 (*Congressional Globe*, 41st Congress, 2nd Session 2845-46).

[94]   The railroad-based timber companies have gained title to land not only through direct grants and purchases, but also through exchanges with the government. See, for example, the Weyerhaeuser section of this book.

THE LAND-GRANT TIMBER CORPORATIONS

THE FOUR LAND-GRANT TIMBER CORPORATIONS COMPARED

The main timber beneficiaries of the Northern Pacific railroad land grant are the companies Plum Creek, Weyerhaeuser, Potlatch, and Boise Cascade, because much of their Pacific Northwest timber land holdings derive from the Northern Pacific land grant. Below is a brief comparison of the four companies, followed by a historical and corporate outline of each.

Table 1. The Land-Grant Corporations Compared [95]

	Assets	Market Value	Average Sales	Average Profits	Acres Claimed	Timber Claimed	Employees	Mills
Plum Creek	817	n/a	398	49	2.1	10.4	1,500	10
Weyerhaeuser	12,683	9,742	9,343	305	23.5	294.0	36,748	140
Potlatch	2,067	1,357	1,283	75	1.5	n/a	7,000	23
Boise Cascade	4,513	988	4,030	-8	6.1	8.9	17,362	43
Total	20,080	12,087	15,054	421	33.2	313.3	62,610	216

[95]   Notes: All financial data are in millions of U.S. dollars. ASSETS are those claimed by each company at year-end 1993. MARKET VALUE is based on stock value on Feb. 28, 1994. SALES and PROFITS are the annual average for the years 1989-1993. ACRES are in millions. Weyerhaeuser acreage includes 18.8 million acres under long-term lease in Canada. Boise Cascade acreage includes 3.3 million acres under long-term lease. TIMBER CLAIMED is sawtimber in billion board feet equivalents, and may not include some pulpwood inventories. Weyerhaeuser timber claimed consists of 104 bbf (billion board feet) in the U.S. and 190 bbf in

BURLINGTON NORTHERN AND PLUM CREEK

A 1988 court settlement removed the lien on grant lands mortgaged by J.P. Morgan's 1896 Northern Pacific bonds. Burlington Northern, corporate successor to Northern Pacific, then spun off Burlington Resources. In 1989 Burlington Resources spun off Plum Creek, which was the company's logging and milling arm, as a limited partnership (L.P.). The name "Plum Creek" came from the name of a small mill in Columbia Falls, Montana, which Burlington Northern had purchased in 1969.

In the spin-off, 88 percent of the L.P. units (essentially, the stock) were offered to the public. The other 12 percent were held by management.[96] Management also held 5 percent of the mills.[97] The holding of 7 percent of a corporation's stock is generally considered sufficient to control the corporation.[98]

The spin-off of Plum Creek raised capital from the public and has had tremendous tax advantages. Plum Creek's establishment as a limited partnership allows the company to take advantage of a portion of the 1987 tax code which exempts natural resource-extracting limited partnerships from paying federal income tax.[99] The partners (shareholders) claim that even 90 percent of their dividends are tax-

---

Canada (1993 Form 10-K, p.5). Plum Creek timber data is calculated from its 1990-1992 Annual Reports, plus the addition of the estimated 2.4 billion board feet on land purchased from Champion International in 1993. Boise Cascade timber does not include 66 million cords of pulpwood. MILLS is the number of major lumber, plywood, paneling, paper, and packaging-manufacturing facilities; there may be more than one facility at a particular location.

Sources: the 1990-1993 Annual Reports and Forms 10-K of each corporation; the *Business Week* 1000 (March 28, 1994) is the source for MARKET VALUES. Complete citations for data in this table are contained in the footnotes for each company's profile (below).

[96]   Since then, management has increased its share. (Plum Creek, 1992 Annual Report, p.22.)

[97]   Plum Creek, May 1989, p.7.

[98]   The U.S. Securities Exchange Commission requires that anyone who acquires 5 percent or more of a company's stock make public this information (SEC Rule 13d).

[99]   Plum Creek's interpretation is based on the Internal Revenue Code of 1986, as amended, Section 7704 (Plum Creek, May 1989, pp.86-88).

free as well.[100] Plum Creek had an effective tax rate in 1992 of 1.5 percent, 93 percent of which was state tax.[101]

As a leveraged buy-out that would make the company less attractive to Wall Street raiders, the spin-off immediately left Plum Creek with a long-term debt of $325 million, but also that amount of cash. Much of this "debt" was owed to its corporate parent, Burlington Resources, which was obligated to insure Plum Creek's dividends until June 1994.[102] Burlington Resources netted from this transaction $266 million in 1989 and $21 million in 1990.[103]

In December, 1992, Burlington Resources sold its interest in Plum Creek to SPO Partners.[104] Burlington Resources retained its financial obligations to Plum Creek shareholders until June 1994. It is not yet known to what extent management of land claimed by Plum Creek will be affected by this sale.

What follows is a brief chronology of the management of the land claimed by Plum Creek. In 1910 Northern Pacific had 36 billion board feet of standing timber on some 32 million acres in Washington, Oregon, Idaho, Montana, and California.[105] By the time Burlington Resources was spun off from the railroad in 1988, the amount of timber had been reduced to 10.5 billion board feet on 1.4 million acres in Washington, Idaho, and Montana.[106] This land was located in Montana (842,000 acres), the Washington Cascades (355,000 acres), eastern Washington (96,000 acres), Idaho, (171,000 acres), and Oregon (11,000 acres).[107]

---

[100]   Ramsey, 1989.
[101]   Plum Creek 1992 Annual Report, p.22.
[102]   Plum Creek, May 1989, p.40.
[103]   Burlington Resources, 1990 Annual Report, p.31.
[104]   Grunbaum, Oct. 2, 1992; Virgin, Jan. 5, 1993; and Plum Creek 1992 Annual Report, p.18.
[105]   U.S. Bureau of Corporations, 1913-1914, Part 1, pp.15-17.
[106]   Calculated from data in the 1990, 1991, and 1992 Plum Creek Annual Reports. There are at least three reasons for the dramatic increase in board feet per acre between 1910 and 1988: (1) the inherent inaccuracy in inventorying timber over large acreages; (2) the fact that timber inventories generally count only merchantable species, and many species which are considered merchantable now were not considered such before; and (3) much of the Northern Pacific's land grant was non-forested.
[107]   Plum Creek, 1988.

In 1992 Plum Creek sold 164,000 acres in the Gallatin mountain range of Montana and its Belgrade, Montana sawmill.[108] Income from land sales was $5.9 million in 1990, $10.1 million in 1991, and $20.3 million in 1992.[109] In 1993 Plum Creek purchased 867,000 acres in Montana from Champion International for $260 million. This more than doubled the amount of land claimed by Plum Creek in Montana and effectively ended Champion's operations in that state.[110]

Ironically, Champion's operations in Montana were also based on Northern Pacific grant lands. In 1907 Northern Pacific sold more than a million acres to the Amalgamated Copper Company (soon to become Anaconda Copper),[111] which was also in the timber business and had mills at Bonner, Montana.[112] By 1910 Amalgamated and Northern Pacific (along with "four relatively small holders") held 79.3 percent of the privately owned timber in Montana.[113] In mid-1972 Champion International purchased Anaconda's lumber operation, including control of 670,500 acres of Montana forestland, for $117 million.[114] This land was included in the 1993 sale of 867,000 acres of land in Montana to Plum Creek.[115] Thus, much of the Montana land granted to Northern Pacific has been returned to one of its corporate descendants.

---

[108]   The buyers were Big Sky Lumber and Moonlight Basin Ranch; the sale price was $24 million (Dow Jones, Aug. 5, 1992).

[109]   Plum Creek, 1992 Annual Report, p.26.

[110]   Dow Jones, July 19, 1993 and Nov. 2, 1993.

[111]   U.S. Bureau of Corporations, 1913-1914, Part 1, pp.234,241; and Schwennesen, July 21, 1993. The sale was actually to a subsidiary of Amalgamated Copper Company. (Part 1, p.18.)

[112]   Malone, Roeder, and Lang, 1991, p.325.

[113]   U.S. Bureau of Corporations, 1913-1914, Part 1, p.153. Plum Creek now owns 90 percent of the timber industry land in Montana (calculated from Plum Creek, 1988; Dow Jones, Aug. 5, 1992; and Dow Jones, Nov. 2, 1993; and Waddell, et al, 1989, p.23).

[114]   Malone, Roeder, and Lang, 1991, pp.325-326.

[115]   Champion has controlled lands granted to Northern Pacific in other states, as well. In 1988 Champion bought the St. Regis paper company for $1.6 billion. Previously, St. Regis had acquired 80,000 acres of Washington state forestland from the St. Paul & Tacoma Lumber Company, which had in 1887 bought the land from Northern Pacific. More recently, title to this land has been sold to the James River Corporation (Steen, 1969, p.62, citing Cox, 1937, p.5; and Morgan, 1982).

By the end of 1990 Plum Creek had nine billion board feet of timber left.[116] In 1991 the company cut 563 million board feet,[117] and in 1992 it cut 469 million board feet,[118] leaving about eight billion board feet. The land Plum Creek purchased from Champion contains an estimated 2.4 billion board feet.[119] As Plum Creek Chairman David Leland has acknowledged, "[T]he company is cutting over lands faster than can be sustained in the long run."[120]

Table 2. Plum Creek Corporate Statistics

Corporate Address:
PLUM CREEK
First Interstate Bldg. - 23rd floor
999 Third Ave.
Seattle, WA 98104
206-467-3600

Assets:
Total assets are listed at $817 million.[121]

Sales & Profits:
Average sales for the years 1988 through 1993 were $398 million; average net income for the same years was $49 million.[122]

Selected Officers/Directors:[123]
David Leland, Chairman.
Ian B. Davidson, of D.A. Davidson and Co.
William Oberndorf, William Patterson, and John Scully, all of SPO Partners & Company.
George M. Dennison, president of the University of Montana.

Shareholders:
After the 1989 spin-off from Burlington Resources, 88 percent of Plum Creek's limited partnership units were sold to the public, and Burlington Resources held 12 percent of Plum Creek's timberlands and 5 percent of Plum Creek's milling

---

[116] Plum Creek, 1990 Annual Report, insert between p.12 and p.13.
[117] Plum Creek, 1991 10-K, pp.11,18.
[118] Plum Creek, 1992 Annual Report, p.1.
[119] Devlin, Aug. 1, 1993.
[120] Ramsey, Nov. 1987.
[121] Plum Creek, 1993 Annual Report, p.28.
[122] Plum Creek, 1992 and 1993 Annual Reports.
[123] Plum Creek, 1993 Annual Report, p. 32.

facilities.[124] In 1992 SPO Partners bought Burlington Resources' interest in Plum Creek.[125]

Land and Timber Claimed:
2.1 million acres and 10.4 billion board feet.[126]
Plum Creek is the second largest corporate landowner in Washington state.[127] Weyerhaeuser is the largest.

Mills:
Plum Creek has ten manufacturing facilities at seven sites: five sawmills, two plywood mills, a medium density fiberboard plant, a chip plant, and a glue-laminated remanufacturing plant. The sites are in: Montana (Kalispell, Pablo, Columbia Falls, and Polson) and Washington (Arden, Spokane, and Roslyn).[128]

Employees:
1,500.[129]

THE WEYERHAEUSER EMPIRE – WEYERHAEUSER

Despite Congressional intent that grant lands be open to settlement, Northern Pacific sold millions of acres to large corporations. This land in Washington, Oregon, Montana, and Idaho formed the basis for at least three of the Pacific Northwest's major timber corporations – Weyerhaeuser, Potlatch, and Boise Cascade.

Throughout their history, these companies have been tightly connected. Despite the fact that interlocking directorates between two or more competing corporations were banned by Section 8 of the Clayton Act (1914),[130] many descendants of Frederick Weyerhaeuser and his associates have been directors of at least two of the three companies simultaneously.

---

[124]   Plum Creek, May 1989, p.7.
[125]   Grunbaum, Oct. 2, 1992; Virgin, Oct. 3, 1992; Virgin, Jan. 5, 1993; and Plum Creek, 1993 Annual Report, p.18.
[126]   Calculated from data in the 1990, 1991, and 1992 Plum Creek Annual Reports, plus the 2.4 billion board feet purchased from Champion (Devlin, Aug. 1, 1993).
[127]   Thomas, 1990.
[128]   Plum Creek, 1993 Annual Report, p. 13.
[129]   Plum Creek, 1993 Annual Report, p.13.
[130]   Section 8 is rarely enforced. Between 1914 and 1965 the Department of Justice and the Federal Trade Commission filed only 23 cases to enforce the section. The Department of Justice cases were cease and desist civil suits, merely asking defendants to abandon interlocks before the trial (Green et al., 1972, pp.313-314).

In the past ten years, the direct interlocks have disappeared, but the family ties and shareholders-in-common remain. For example, Potlatch still has directors from the Weyerhaeuser family, and nearly half its stock is controlled by Weyerhaeuser-associated interests.[131] The Laird Norton Trust, associated with Weyerhaeuser since the 1800s, is still a major stockholder in all three companies.[132]

These connections have historically had significant impact on the public. For example, these corporations were involved in the 1970s paper and plywood price-fixing cases brought by the U.S. Department of Justice and by the Federal Trade Commission. Weyerhaeuser was fined $54 million, Boise Cascade $26 million, and Potlatch $10 million.[133]

This oligopoly was created with lands drawn from the public trust – most of Frederick Weyerhaeuser's holdings in the Pacific Northwest were purchased from Northern Pacific.[134] Much of the land eventually titled to Weyerhaeuser in Oregon was acquired by Northern Pacific in the Mt. Rainier National Park exchange: Northern Pacific received its choice of prime timberlands in any states within which Northern Pacific ran track in exchange for the lands which became the Mt. Rainier Forest Reserve.[135] The Congressional delegation from Washington state helped to push through the bill that allowed this land exchange to take place, as author Carsten Lien wrote. By 1915, "the

---

[131]   Frederick T. and William T. Weyerhaeuser are directors of Potlatch. Dorfman (1991) and McCoy (1992) claim that Weyerhaeuser interests hold about 40 percent of Potlatch stock.

[132]   As shown in the 1990 Forms 10-K of Weyerhaeuser, Potlatch, and Boise Cascade. The structure of the Weyerhaeuser family organization has been investigated by Dunn (1980).

[133]   Champion International's Hoerner Waldorf division also was fined $47 million for price-fixing in the 1972-1978 paper cases (all from Moskowitz, Katz, and Levering, 1980, p.587).

[134]   One of the most detailed discussions of the transactions between Northern Pacific and Weyerhaeuser is by Hidy, Hill, and Nevins, 1963; see pp.105-106,190,215,222,224,227,250,252, and 268. See also the U.S. Bureau of Corporations, 1913-1914.

[135]   Now the Mt. Baker Snoqualmie and Gifford Pinchot National Forests. The laws establishing Rainier as a Forest Reserve and then as a National Park, and giving Northern Pacific in-lieu lands elsewhere include: the Sundry Civil Appropriations Act (30 Stat. 34, June 4, 1897) as later amended (30 Stat. 597, July 1, 1898) and by the act of May 17, 1906 (34 Stat. 197).

enormity of the public loss was common knowledge."[136] As Congressman Thomson of Illinois later described it, "Mountain peaks, barren hillsides, lava beds, swamp lands and other valueless holdings. . . were released and the most valuable timber, coal and oil lands within the public lands were taken in exchange. . . . The bars were let down for wholesale fraud and a national scandal resulted."[137] The result of this scandal was that Frederick Weyerhaeuser and his associates gained title to hundreds of thousands of acres of land in the Pacific Northwest.

Since the turn of the century, the Weyerhaeuser Company has cut four million acres (almost 6,320 square miles) and replanted 3.4 million acres (5,355 square miles). In 1992 alone, Weyerhaeuser cut 45 square miles in Washington, 25 square miles in Oregon, and 152 square miles in the southern U.S.[138]

This much cutting has had a dramatic effect on the forests of the Pacific Northwest. When Frederick Weyerhaeuser began cutting over the railroad grant lands he had received from Northern Pacific, most of the forest was in excess of 300 years old.[139] Now, Weyerhaeuser claims to have virtually no old growth left.[140] Further, if Weyerhaeuser cuts at its current claimed rate of 2 percent per year,[141] the maximum age for the trees in its plantations would be 50 years, and the average age would be approximately 25 years. Reducing the average age of the trees over extensive landscapes in the Pacific Northwest by more than 83 percent has been another unintended result of the 1864 Northern Pacific land grant.

Table 3. Weyerhaeuser Corporate Statistics

Corporate Address:
WEYERHAEUSER
33663 Weyerhaeuser Drive South
Federal Way, WA 98003
206-924-2345

---

[136] Lien, 1991, pp. 9-15.
[137] Quoted in Lien, 1991, p. 15, citing *Congressional Record* 322:2147.
[138] Weyerhaeuser, 1992 Form 10-K, p.6.
[139] Harris, (1984, p.11), citing early inventories by the U.S. Forest Service (1940) and the Pacific Northwest Loggers Association (1946).
[140] Norse, 1990, pp.247-248; and Taylor and Werner, Nov. 10, 1990.
[141] Weyerhaeuser, July 24, 1990; and Aug. 7, 1990.

Assets:
$12.683 billion at the end of FY 1993.[142]

Sales & Profits:
Average annual sales and profits from 1989 through 1993 were $9.3 billion and $305 million; in 1991 Weyerhaeuser lost $162 million on sales of $8.8 billion.[143] This loss, the company's first since 1933, was due to real estate losses, plant closures and modernization, and environmental cleanup costs.[144] Weyerhaeuser exports approximately one of three logs unprocessed.[145] Raw materials sales, including logs, chips, and timber, were worth $1 billion in 1993.[146]

Selected Officers/Directors:[147]
George H. Weyerhaeuser.
William H. Clapp (member of family associated with Weyerhaeuser since the 1800s).
W. John Driscoll (member of family associated with Weyerhaeuser since the 1800s).
E. Bronson Ingram (member of family associated with Weyerhaeuser since the 1800s).
William D. Ruckleshaus (former Administrator of the U.S. Environmental Protection Agency).

Shareholders:[148]
54 percent of Weyerhaeuser's stock is held by institutions.
Laird-Norton Trust (1,128,367 shares in June 1991).
George H. Weyerhaeuser (2,992,404 shares in Jan. 1991).
William H. Clapp (331,912 shares in Jan. 1991).
W. John Driscoll (3,951,909 shares in Jan. 1991).
E. Bronson Ingram (374,808 shares in Jan. 1991).
Total held by directors and officers (12,458,314 shares in Jan. 1991).

Land and Timber Claimed:
Weyerhaeuser claims approximately 5.6 million acres in the southern and northwestern United States, and has long-term license arrangements to 17.8 million acres in Canada.[149] In 1991 the company estimated its timber inventory on U.S. land to be 104 billion board feet and on Canadian land to be 190 billion board feet.[150]

---

[142] Weyerhaeuser, 1993 Annual Report, p.46.
[143] Weyerhaeuser, 1993 Annual Report, p.45; and 1991 Annual Report, p. 33.
[144] Virgin, Jan. 4, 1992; and Weyerhaeuser, 1991, Annual Report, p.20.
[145] Weyerhaeuser, Nov./Dec. 1991.
[146] Weyerhaeuser, 1992 Annual Report, p.23.
[147] Weyerhaeuser, 1993 Annual Report, p.78.
[148] Weyerhaeuser, 1990 10-K Form; and Weyerhaeuser, 1990 Annual Report, p.3; and *Business Week 1000*, March 28, 1994, p. 83.
[149] Weyerhaeuser, 1993 Form 10-K, p.5.
[150] Weyerhaeuser, 1993 Form 10-K, p.5.

Mills:
Weyerhaeuser has 140 major lumber, plywood, paneling, paper, recycling, chemical and packaging facilities.[151]

Employees:[152]
36,748.

THE WEYERHAEUSER EMPIRE – POTLATCH

Potlatch was incorporated in 1903 by Weyerhaeuser, Peter Musser, and Laird Norton.[153] It was started with Northern Pacific land grant in-lieu scrip from the 1899 legislation creating Mt. Rainier National Park and with direct purchases from the Northern Pacific.[154] In 1931 it combined with two other Weyerhaeuser-associated companies, Clearwater Timber and Edward Rutledge Timber.[155] Members of the Weyerhaeuser, Jewett, or Davis families comprised all of the presidents of Potlatch from 1903 to the 1960s.[156]

Table 4. Potlatch Corporate Statistics

Corporate Address:
POTLATCH
One Maritime Plaza
San Francisco, CA 94111
415-576-8800

Assets:
$2.067 billion at end of FY 1993.[157]

Sales & Profits:
Potlatch's 1989-1993 average annual sales were $1.283 billion; its average profits were $75 million.[158]

Officers/Directors:[159]
Frederick T. Weyerhaeuser.

---

[151]   Weyerhaeuser, 1993 Annual Report, pp.26, 30.
[152]   Weyerhaeuser, 1993 Annual Report, p.76.
[153]   Hidy, Hill, and Nevins, 1963, p.255.
[154]   Hidy, Hill, and Nevins, 1963, pp.250,252; and U.S. Bureau of Corporations, 1913-1914.
[155]   Hidy, Hill, and Nevins, 1963, p.435.
[156]   Hidy, Hill, and Nevins, 1963, pp.591,661.
[157]   Potlatch, 1993 Annual Report, p.37.
[158]   Potlatch, 1993 Annual Report, p.48.
[159]   Potlatch, 1993 Annual Report, p.52.

William T. Weyerhaeuser.

George F. Jewett, Jr. (member of a family associated with Weyerhaeuser since the 1800s).

Shareholders:[160]

39 percent of Potlatch's stock is held by institutions.

Some 40 percent of Potlatch stock is owned by Weyerhaeuser associates.[161] These include:

Weyerhaeuser-associated Laird Norton Trust (91,175 shares in September 1993).

George F. Jewett, Jr., member of family associated with Weyerhaeuser since the 1800s (1,390,818 shares in December 1990).

Frederick Davis (44,224 shares in May 1987).

J. P. Weyerhaeuser III (116,272 shares in September 1992).

Frederick T. Weyerhaeuser (54,500 shares in August 1989).

WBW Trust (39,500 shares in April, 1992).

Land and Timber Claimed:

Potlatch claims 1.5 million acres of pine, fir, and aspen in Arkansas (504,000), Minnesota (318,000), and Idaho (678,000).[162] The amount of timber claimed is not disclosed in its annual report.

Mills:[163]

Potlatch owns 23 saw, plywood, particleboard, pulp, paper and tissue mills.

Employees:[164]

7,000.

THE WEYERHAEUSER EMPIRE – BOISE CASCADE

This company was first incorporated by Weyerhaeuser in 1913 as Boise Payette.[165] Boise Payette and Cascade Lumber (Yakima, Washington) were merged in 1957 into Boise Cascade.[166] Norton Clapp was president from 1949 until the 1960s, and directors included Weyerhaeusers and the Weyerhaeuser-associated families of Mussers, Clapps, Titcombs, and Jewetts.[167]

---

[160] Potlatch, 1991 and 1992 10-K Form; and *Business Week 1000*, March 28, 1994, p. 83.

[161] Dorfman, 1991; and McCoy, 1992.

[162] Potlatch, 1993 Annual Report, p.28.

[163] Potlatch, 1993 Annual Report, p.27.

[164] Potlatch, 1993 Annual Report, p.48.

[165] Hidy, Hill, and Nevins, 1963, p.265.

[166] *Hoover's Handbook of American Business 1992*, p.149.

[167] Hidy, Hill, and Nevins, 1963, p.658.

Table 5. Boise Cascade Corporate Statistics

Corporate Address:
BOISE CASCADE
One Jefferson Square
Boise, ID 83702
208-384-6161

Assets:
Boise Cascade claimed a net worth of $4.513 billion at the end of 1993.[168]

Sales & Profits:
Average sales from 1989 to 1993 were $4.030 billion; it lost an average of $8 million.[169] Boise Cascade, like Potlatch, gets most of its revenues and profits from paper products.[170] In 1993 half of its sales were from paper products; 40 percent was from building products.[171]

Selected Officers/Directors:[172]
James McClure, former U.S. Senator from Idaho.
Anne Armstrong, former U.S. Ambassador to Great Britain and counselor to the
        President of the U.S.
Frank Shrontz, chairman and CEO of Boeing.
Edson Spencer, former chairman and CEO of Honeywell.

Shareholders:[173]
62 percent of Boise Cascade stock is held by institutions.
Weyerhaeuser-associated Laird-Norton Trust (67,172 shares in September 1993).
Edward R. Titcomb, member of family associated with Weyerhaeuser since the
        1800s (50,340 shares in December 1987).

Land and Timber Claimed:
Boise Cascade owns or controls 6.1 million acres in Canada and the U.S.; 1.3 million acres are in the Pacific Northwest.[174] Boise Cascade claims 8.9 billion board feet of sawtimber inventory and 66 million cords of pulpwood.[175]

Mills:[176]
Boise Cascade has 43 pulp and paper, corrugated container, plywood and veneer, particle board, and saw mills.

---

[168]   Boise Cascade, 1993 Annual Report, p.40.
[169]   Boise Cascade, 1993 Annual Report, p.39.
[170]   Boise Cascade, 1993 Annual Report, p. 39.
[171]   Boise Cascade, 1993 Annual Report, p. 39.
[172]   Boise Cascade, 1993 Annual Report, p. 50.
[173]   Boise Cascade, 1990-1992 Forms 10-K and 10-Q.
[174]   Boise Cascade, 1992 Annual Report, p.49.
[175]   Boise Cascade, 1992 Annual Report, p.49.
[176]   Boise Cascade, 1993 Annual Report, pp. 44-48.

Boise Cascade has increased its mill capacity in the southern U.S. by 475 percent during the 1980s.[177]

Employees:[178]
17,362.

CONCLUSION

As corporations beholden to shareholders, the Northern Pacific land-grant-based timber companies have maximized profits. As this book will demonstrate, the liquidation of forests for maximized profits has damaged and continues to damage the forests and the forest-dependent communities of the Pacific Northwest. Much of the land claimed by Plum Creek, Weyerhaeuser, Potlatch, and Boise Cascade was conditionally granted to Northern Pacific by Congress to raise capital to build and maintain a railroad. Northern Pacific improperly retained title to this land through two financial collapses and it became the foundation of many timber empires. The next section explores the effects of these timber empires' management policies on the forests and communities of the Pacific Northwest.

---

[177] Anderson and Olson, 1991, p.49.
[178] Boise Cascade, 1993 Annual Report, p.42.

RAILROADS AND CLEARCUTS

LEGACY OF CONGRESS'S
1864 NORTHERN PACIFIC RAILROAD LAND GRANT

A Photographic Essay

© Trygve Steen

"... Congress may, at any time, having due regard for the rights of said Northern Pacific Railroad Company, add to, alter, amend, or repeal this act."

— Section 20,
1864 Northern Pacific Railroad Land Grant

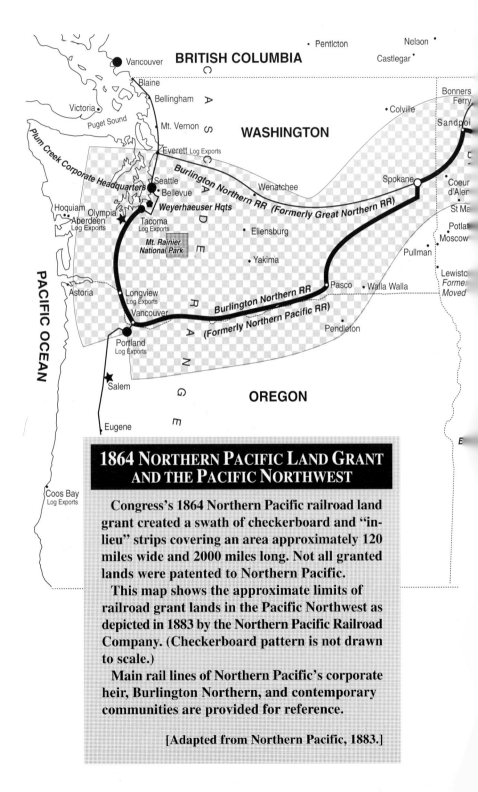

Penticton
Nelson
Vancouver
BRITISH COLUMBIA
Castlegar

Blaine
Bonners Ferry
Victoria
Bellingham
CASCA
Colville
Puget Sound
Mt. Vernon
Sandpoi
WASHINGTON
Everett Log Exports
Plum Creek Corporate Headquarters
Burlington Northern RR (Formerly Great Northern RR)
Seattle
Bellevue
Wenatchee
Spokane
Coeur d'Aler
Hoquiam
Weyerhaeuser Hqts
St Ma
Olympia
Aberdeen
Log Exports
Tacoma
Log Exports
Ellensburg
Potlat
Moscow
Mt. Rainier
National Park
Yakima
Pullman
Astoria
Longview
Log Exports
Pasco
Walla Walla
Lewisto
Forme:
Moved
Vancouver
Burlington Northern RR
(Formerly Northern Pacific RR)
Pendleton
Portland
Log Exports
Salem
OREGON
Eugene

Coos Bay
Log Exports

1864 NORTHERN PACIFIC LAND GRANT AND THE PACIFIC NORTHWEST

Congress's 1864 Northern Pacific railroad land grant created a swath of checkerboard and "in-lieu" strips covering an area approximately 120 miles wide and 2000 miles long. Not all granted lands were patented to Northern Pacific.

This map shows the approximate limits of railroad grant lands in the Pacific Northwest as depicted in 1883 by the Northern Pacific Railroad Company. (Checkerboard pattern is not drawn to scale.)

Main rail lines of Northern Pacific's corporate heir, Burlington Northern, and contemporary communities are provided for reference.

[Adapted from Northern Pacific, 1883.]

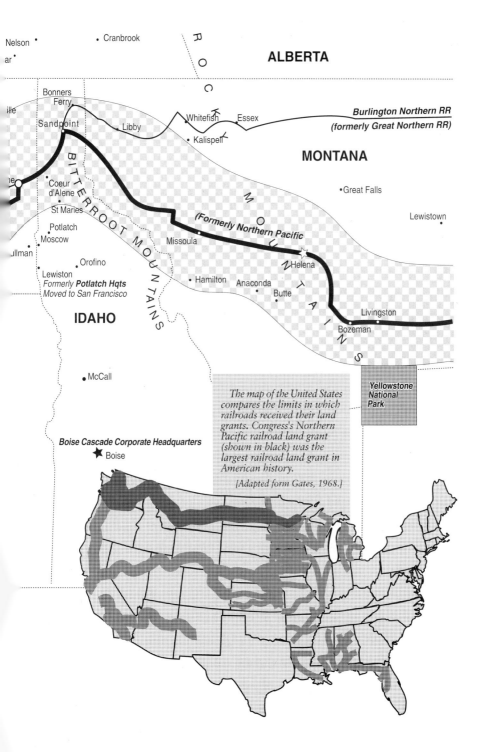

Nelson

ar

Cranbrook

ROCKY

ALBERTA

Bonners
Ferry

ille

Sandpoint

Libby

Whitefish   Essex

Kalispell

Burlington Northern RR
(formerly Great Northern RR)

MONTANA

ne

Coeur
d'Alene

BITTERROOT

St Maries

Potlatch

Moscow

ullman

Orofino

Lewiston
Formerly **Potlatch Hqts**
Moved to San Francisco

IDAHO

M
O
U
N
T
A
I
N
S

(Formerly Northern Pacific

Missoula

Hamilton

Anaconda

Butte

Helena

Great Falls

Lewistown

Livingston

Bozeman

McCall

Yellowstone
National
Park

Boise Cascade Corporate Headquarters
Boise

*The map of the United States
compares the limits in which
railroads received their land
grants. Congress's Northern
Pacific railroad land grant
(shown in black) was the
largest railroad land grant in
American history.*
[Adapted form Gates, 1968.]

FORESTS AND THE
1864 NORTHERN PACIFIC LAND GRANT
CONGRESS'S SUBSIDY TO BUILD AND MAINTAIN A RAILROAD

IEPLC

Checkerboard forest clearcut by Plum Creek Timber Company, Colville National Forest in northeastern Washington. Aerial views of Pacific Northwest forests reveal the checkerboard pattern that is a legacy of Congress's Northern Pacific railroad land grant. This same clearcut is pictured to the right, as seen from the ground.

IEPLC

In the Pacific Northwest, the land grant's checkerboard pattern on forest maps has become a reality in the forest.

LAND GRANT LEGACY:
THE CHECKERBOARD FORESTS

Chief Sitting Bull (1834-90)

Chief Sitting Bull (Tatonka I Yatanka), leader of the Sioux nation, said in his language at a ceremony marking the completion of the Northern Pacific's main line in 1883, "I hate you. I hate you. I hate all the white people. You are thieves and liars. You have taken away our land and made us outcasts, so I hate you." Sitting Bull's words were translated into a friendly, courteous speech for the audience (Glaspell, 1941).

National Archives Collection

President Abraham Lincoln (1809-65)

In 1864 Congress and President Lincoln created Northern Pacific and conditionally granted it 40 million acres of the public domain for the purpose of raising capital to build and maintain a railroad from Lake Superior to the Pacific Ocean.

Dictionary of American Portraits, Courtesy New York Historical Society

CONGRESS AND THE CHECKERBOARDS

Congress's 1864 Northern Pacific land grant created a swath of checkerboard lands nearly 2000 miles long and up to 120 miles wide between Lake Superior and the Pacific Ocean.

For every mile of track built, Congress conditionally granted Northern Pacific 40 square miles of public lands in the Western Territories.

Congress also allowed NP to select lands in special "indemnity belts" located at the outer reaches of the checkerboard. These belts were 20 miles wide.

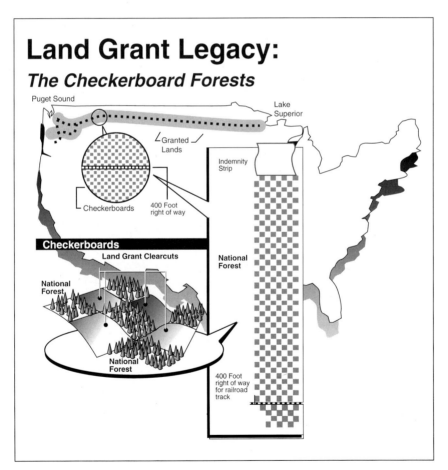

Land Grant Legacy:
The Checkerboard Forests

Puget Sound

Lake Superior

Granted Lands

Indemnity Strip

Checkerboards

400 Foot right of way

Checkerboards

Land Grant Clearcuts

National Forest

National Forest

National Forest

National Forest

400 Foot right of way for railroad track

WESTERN TERRITORIES:
INTO THE HANDS OF ROBBER BARONS

Dictionary of American Portraits

Jay Cooke,
Investment Banker
(1821-1905)

In 1870 Cooke, head of the nation's largest banking house, used his money to "gain the votes of recalcitrant Congressmen" to rewrite Congress's 1864 contract, allowing Northern Pacific to sell bonds rather than stocks. In 1873 Northern Pacific failed, taking Cooke with it and helping to trigger a nationwide depression. (Schwinden, 1950, and Sobel, 1988.)

Frederick Weyerhaeuser,
Lumber Magnate
(1834-1914)

In 1899 James J. Hill sold to Weyerhaeuser nearly a million acres of Northern Pacific grant lands. This was Weyerhaeuser's largest of several purchases. Most of Weyerhaeuser's holdings in the Pacific Northwest derive from the Northern Pacific land grant. (U.S. Bureau of Corporations, 1913-14.)

Dictionary of American Portraits, Courtesy Weyerhaeuser Company

J. P. Morgan and James J. Hill

J. P. Morgan, Financier (1837-1913)

Dictionary of American Portraits, Courtesy of Library of Congress

Financial panic in 1893 swept Northern Pacific into receivership. After this, Morgan and Hill effectively combined the "northern" lines (Northern Pacific and Great Northern), added the Chicago Burlington & Quincy Railroad in 1901, and formed the framework for the Burlington Northern Railroad.

James J. Hill, Railroad Promoter, Financier (1838-1916)

In 1893 James J. Hill completed the Great Northern Railroad, linking St. Paul, Minnesota, with Everett, Washington. In the Pacific Northwest's era of railroad building, Hill became known as the Empire Builder. "Give me enough Swedes and whiskey and I'll build a railroad through Hell," he reputedly said (Schwantes, 1993, p. 133). Hill associated closely with J.P. Morgan and Frederick Weyerhaeuser.

Dictionary of American Portraits, Photograph by Pach Brothers

MORGAN, HILL, AND THE
BURLINGTON NORTHERN RAILROAD
COMBINING THE TWO NORTHERN LINES AND THE BURLINGTON

Northern Pacific Railroad

In the 1890s Morgan and Hill effectively combined Northern Pacific with the parallel and competing Great Northern.

Great Northern Railroad

Burlington Railroad

The purchase of the Chicago Burlington & Quincy Railroad gave Morgan and Hill rail access to lucrative markets in Chicago and St. Louis, and triggered a battle with Harriman of Union Pacific that caused panic in the nation's stock markets in 1901.

Burlington Northern Railroad

Morgan's and Hill's efforts to form a railroad monopoly, beginning in the 1890s, were repeatedly struck down by the Supreme Court. In 1970 the Supreme Court acceded to the merger, and Burlington Northern was created.

Burlington Northern is the nation's longest railroad, with over 24,000 miles of track. Burlington Northern links Puget Sound to the Great Lakes, and links Canada to Gulf Coast ports in Texas, Alabama, and Florida.

CHRONOLOGY

1864 Congress passes the Northern Pacific (NP) land grant, creating Northern Pacific Railroad Company. Congress conditionally grants 40 million acres of public lands in a checkerboard pattern to subsidize railroad construction and maintenance.

1870 Congress amends the NP land grant, allowing NP to sell bonds. Construction begins.

1873 NP fails, triggering a national financial panic.

1883 NP completes the main line, seven years after the original deadline.

1890 Congress revests railroad grant lands, including two million acres of the NP grant. NP sells 212,722 acres in Minnesota to Weyerhaeuser.

1893 NP fails financially a second time. James J. Hill completes Great Northern's (GN) main line.

1894 J.P. Morgan and James J. Hill combine NP and GN.

1896 Minnesota and U.S. Supreme Courts rule against merger of NP and GN. Morgan refinances NP with 100- and 150-year bonds.

1899 Congress establishes Mt. Rainier National Park, enabling NP to exchange "rocks and ice" for other public lands.
NP begins to sell granted lands in Washington, Oregon, and Idaho to Weyerhaeuser and associates. By 1940 over 1.5 million acres have been sold to Weyerhaeuser and associates.

1901 Morgan and Hill acquire the Burlington Railroad.

1903 Weyerhaeuser and associates incorporate Potlatch.

1904 U.S. Supreme Court strikes down merger of NP and GN.

1906 NP claims lands already protected in the Gallatin National Forest, near Yellowstone Park.

1907 NP sells about 1 million acres in Montana to Amalgamated Copper (later named Anaconda Copper).

1913 Weyerhaeuser incorporates Boise Payette.

1916 Congress revests three million acres of the O & C (Oregon & California) railroad grant lands in Oregon.

1924 President Coolidge asks Congress to investigate NP.
Congress soon begins investigating the NP land grant. The investigation continues to 1928.

1929 President Hoover signs a bill directing the U. S. Attorney General to sue NP for the return of 2.8 million acres.

1930 U.S. Attorney General files suit in Spokane against NP.

1931 Potlatch joined with Clearwater and Rutledge Timber Companies.

1940 Supreme Court hears United States v. Northern Pacific.

1941 Partial settlement between NP and U.S. Attorney General returns 2.8 million acres to the national forests.

1957 Boise Payette joined with Cascade Lumber to form Boise Cascade.

1970 Supreme Court allows the merger of the Burlington and the two northern lines (NP and GN), thereby forming Burlington Northern (BN).

1981 BN reorganizes as a holding company.

1988 Liens on J. P. Morgan's bonds are lifted by a settlement with the bondholders, allowing the railroad's grant lands and natural resources to be spun off into Burlington Resources.

1989 Burlington Resources spins off Plum Creek Timber Company.

1992 SPO Partners acquires control of Plum Creek, a tax-free limited partnership since 1988.

1993 Plum Creek purchases 867,000 acres of western Montana timberland from Champion International, which had purchased it from Anaconda Copper in 1972, which had purchased it from NP in 1907.

WEYERHAEUSER COMES TO THE PACIFIC NORTHWEST

MT. RAINIER SCRIP AND LAKE STATES LUMBERMEN

Frederick Weyerhauser emerged as the nation's preeminent lumberman by logging forests of the Midwest during the late 1800s.

By the turn of the century, the end was near for the once vast pine forests of the Great Lakes region and upper Mississippi River Valley.

James J. Hill was one of Weyerhaeuser's neighbors in St. Paul, spending many evenings at the Weyerhaeuser home. In 1899 Hill sold to Weyerhaeuser nearly a million acres of Northern Pacific grant lands in the Pacific Northwest. Weyerhaeuser, along with other Lake States lumbermen, then shifted operations from the cutover forests of the Midwest to the Pacific Northwest.

Not all of the Northern Pacific grant lands were rich forests. Some were "rocks and ice." But Congress helped Morgan and Hill by creating the Mt. Rainier National Park: a "rider" in the law gave Northern Pacific the option of exchanging nearly a million acres of checkerboards in the Mt. Rainier Forest Reserve (now parts of the Gifford Pinchot National Forest and Mt. Baker-Snoqualmie National Forest) for public lands elsewhere. This "Mt. Rainier scrip" was used by the Weyerhaeuser syndicate to exchange Cascade Range rocks and ice for control of rich forests elsewhere, including Idaho and Oregon.

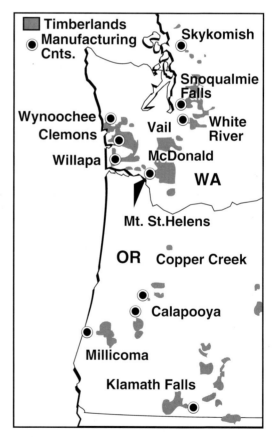

Weyerhaeuser's timber holdings in Washington and Oregon, 1959. Most of these lands are based on the Northern Pacific contracts (adapted from Fortune, *July 1959, v.60, no. 1, p. 93).*

Mark Lawler

Mt. Rainier

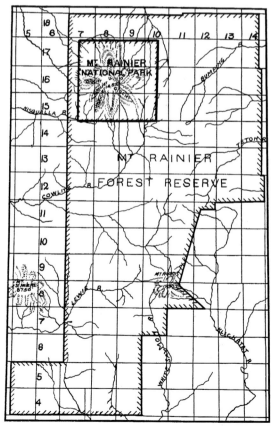

"Map of the Mt. Rainier Forest Reserve, showing the position of the Mt. Rainier National Park, which was created for the special benefit of the Northern Pacific Railroad Company, that the Hill corporation might be enabled to exchange its worthless holdings for the cream of creation."

(From Puter and Stevens, 1908.)

WESTERN WASHINGTON AND NORTHERN PACIFIC

Map showing checkerboard pattern of timberland ownership deriving from the Northern Pacific Railroad land grant. (U.S. Bureau of Corporations, 1913-1914, Part 2, p. 44.) Weyerhaeuser holdings on this map totaled 1,372,474 acres, containing an estimated 70 billion board feet; nearly 90 percent of this was acquired from the Northern Pacific. Northern Pacific holdings include 306,261 acres, containing an estimated 11 billion board feet.

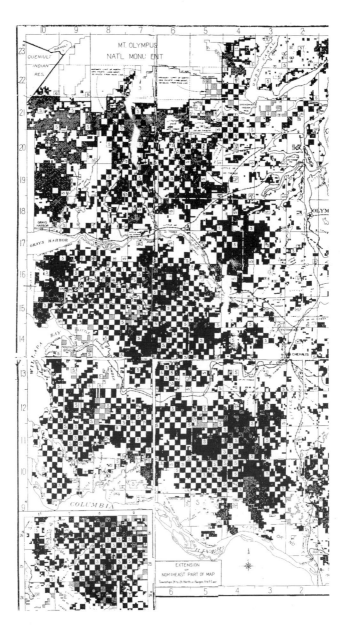

The "Group Of Large Holdings" (holding 731,803 acres with 40 billion board feet) is comprised of 33 companies, including Chicago, Milwaukee & St. Paul Railway, St. Paul & Tacoma Lumber, Puget Mill, Simpson, Merrill-Ring, Polson Logging, Western Timber, Great Northern Railway, and others; Weyerhaeuser and Northern Pacific held interests in some of these companies (U.S. Bureau of Corporations, 1913-1914, Part 2, pp. 28, 30).

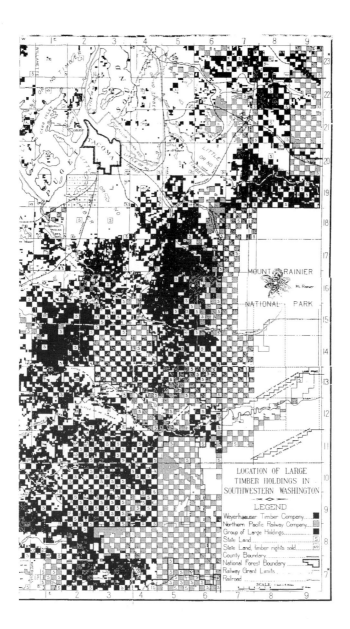

NORTH IDAHO AND NORTHERN PACIFIC

Map showing checkerboard pattern of timberland ownership deriving from the Northern Pacific Railroad land grant (U.S. Bureau of Corporations, 1913-1914, Part 2, p. 130).

Northern Pacific holdings on this map comprise 108,403 acres, containing an estimated 1.6 billion board feet. The "First Group Of Large Holdings" (Potlatch Lumber and Clearwater Timber, largely controlled by Weyerhaeuser interests, and acquiring much of their land from the Northern Pacific; and the Chicago, Milwaukee & St. Paul Railway) is shown on the map with 508,778 acres, containing an estimated 16 billion board feet of timber. The "Second Group Of Large Holdings" (Edward Rutledge Timber, also associated with Weyerhaeuser; Blackwell Lumber; and Coeur d'Alene Lumber) controlled 118,406 acres with 3.4 billion board feet. This second group also largely acquired its land from the Northern Pacific land grant (U.S. Bureau of Corporations, 1913-1914, Part 2, p. 119-124).

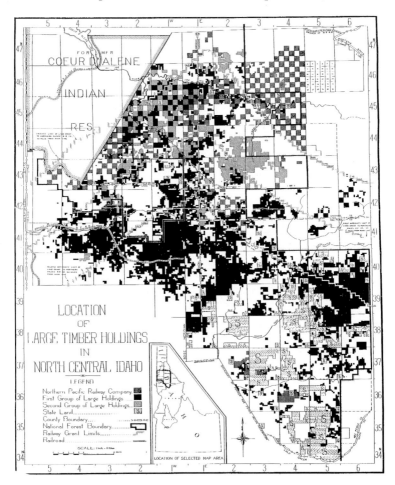

Land Grant Checkerboard Forests: Mallard Larkins Region, Idaho Panhandle National Forests

CONGRESS'S 1864 LAND GRANT AND PATTERNS OF CORPORATE POWER

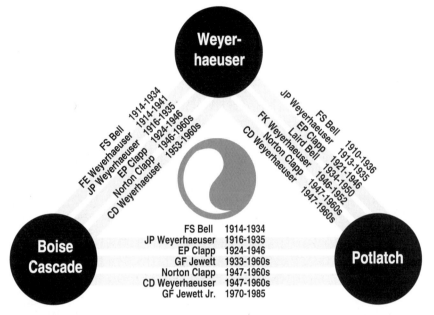

FS Bell	1914-1934
JP Weyerhaeuser	1916-1935
EP Clapp	1924-1946
GF Jewett	1933-1960s
Norton Clapp	1947-1960s
CD Weyerhaeuser	1947-1960s
GF Jewett Jr.	1970-1985

Interlocking boards of directors, selected examples.

(Source: Annual reports of the companies, and Hidy, Hill, and Nevins, 1963, pp. 658 - 665.)

Boise Cascade world headquarters in Boise, Idaho.

Weyerhaeuser world headquarters near Tacoma, Washington, not far from Mt. Rainier National Park.

The Weyerhaeuser syndicate incorporated Potlatch in 1903 to log forests in north Idaho. In 1913 Weyerhaeuser incorporated Boise Payette, which in 1957 was joined with Yakima-based Cascade Lumber to form Boise Cascade.

Potlatch corporate headquarters at One Maritime Plaza in San Francisco, California.

INTERLOCKING CORPORATE OFFICERS AND DIRECTORS (SELECTED EXAMPLES)

Several officers/directors went directly from **Anaconda Copper** to **Burlington Northern** in the early 1980s.

Boise Cascade, Burlington Northern, and **Burlington Resources** were interlocked from 1981 to 1992 by J.B. Parrish.

Boise Cascade, Great Northern, and **Weyerhaeuser** were interlocked from the 1910s to 1940s (through Frederick and F.E. Weyerhaeuser).

Boise Cascade, Northern Pacific, and **Potlatch** were interlocked from 1947 to 1955 by G.F. Jewett.

Boise Cascade, Potlatch, and **Weyerhaeuser** were interlocked from the time of their incorporation by Weyerhaeuser and associates in the early 1900s until the 1980s (through members of the Bell, Clapp, Jewett, Musser, and Weyerhaeuser families).

Burlington Northern and **Weyerhaeuser** were interlocked from 1969 to 1981 (through Robert B. Wilson and through Frederick Weyerhaeuser's great-grandson Walter J. Driscoll).

Burlington Resources and **Weyerhaeuser** were interlocked in 1987 and 1988 (through William Ruckelshaus, who formed Burlington Resources' Ecos - a hazardous waste company - and who has been on the Weyerhaeuser board since 1976).

Northern Pacific, Potlatch, and **Weyerhaeuser** were interlocked from 1935 to 1946 by R.M. Weyerhaeuser.

Potlatch was incorporated by Frederick Weyerhaeuser and associates, and has been interlocked ever since. There are currently two Weyerhaeusers (Frederick T. and William T.) on the Potlatch board. Weyerhaeuser interests are estimated to hold at least 40 percent of the stock of Potlatch.

Selected Corporate Beneficiaries Of The Northern Pacific Land Grants

Northern Pacific (1864, 1870)
38.6 million acres.

Weyerhaeuser (incorporated 1878)
Bought at least 1,489,000 acres from Northern Pacific, 1890-1940.

Potlatch (incorporated 1903)
At least 229,000 land grant in-lieu acres 1901-1927.

Boise Payette (**Boise Cascade**) (incorporated 1913)
At least 172,000 land grant in-lieu acres 1913-1947.

Anaconda (Amalgamated) Copper (**Standard Oil** acq. 1899)
Bought more than 1 million acres from NP by 1910.

Champion International
Bought 670,500 land grant acres from **Anaconda** in 1972;
sold 867,000 acres to **Plum Creek** in 1993.

Burlington Northern (incorporated 1970)
Railroad track: 24,000 miles.

Burlington Resources (spun off 1988)
Glacier Park Real Estate: 925,000 acres.
Meridian Minerals: taconite, talc, dolomite, kaolin.

Plum Creek Timber (spun off 1989)
Timber: 10.4 billion board feet on 2.1 million acres.

Meridian Gold (1990)

Meridian Aggregates (spun off 1991)

Meridian Oil (subsidiary of **Burlington Resources**)
Oil & Gas: 5.7 trillion cu. ft. on 13.3 million acres.

El Paso Natural Gas (spun off 1992)
Natural gas pipeline: 17,000 miles.

Great Northern Properties LP (spun off 1992)
Coal: 16 billion tons.

[Sources: Burlington Northern Railroad, 1992 Annual Report, p.27; Burlington Resources, 1992 Annual Report, p.15; El Paso Natural Gas, Mar. 12. 1992 Prospectus, p.F-4; Plum Creek Timber, 1992 Annual Report, p.16.]

LIQUIDATING THE LAND-GRANT FORESTS
CLEARCUTTING FROM YELLOWSTONE PARK TO SEATTLE

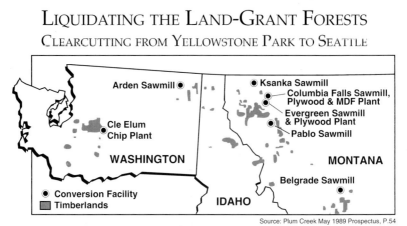

Source: Plum Creek May 1989 Prospectus, P.54

Plum Creek's holdings in 1989 (adapted from Plum Creek's Prospectus, May 1989, p.54). In 1993 its holdings in Montana more than doubled.

By 1980 Morgan and Hill's railroad, the Burlington Northern, still retained about 1.5 million acres of checkerboard forests between Yellowstone Park and the Pacific Ocean. BN's logging arm, Plum Creek, began liquidating the forests in the early 1980s. Plum Creek became a tax-free "limited partnership" in 1989.

In 1907 Hill sold a million acres of the Northern Pacific checkerboard lands in northwestern Montana to Amalgamated Copper, which later became Anaconda Copper. In the 1970s most of this land was sold to Champion International. Champion overcut the forests and in 1993 sold the grant lands to Plum Creek.

Checkerboards. Montana, Mission Mountain Wilderness as backdrop. April 1988.

IEPLC

Checkerboards. Idaho, Mallard Larkins region of the Bitterroot Mountains. June 1989.

Marianne Gordon

Checkerboards. Washington, near Snoqualmie Pass in the Cascade Range. October 1986.

LEGACY OF THE 1864 NORTHERN PACIFIC LAND GRANT

USDA

Checkerboards - an aerial view. Trail Creek, near the Cabinet Wilderness in northwestern Montana, August 1992. The checkerboards in this aerial photograph correspond to the clearcut pictured below.

IEPLC

Checkerboards - as seen from the ground. Champion International and Burlington Northern/Plum Creek severely overcut the forests in northwestern Montana. Throughout American history, overcutting has forced forest-dependent communities into a difficult transition.

Checkerboards. Eastern Washington, Colville National Forest.

Potlatch. Floodwood forest region of the Clearwater River watershed in Idaho, 1992. In Idaho during the early 1900s the Weyerhaeuser syndicate's agents used "Mt. Rainier scrip" to gain control of valuable public forests.

LOG EXPORTS AND CONGRESS'
SUBSTITUTION LOOPHOLE
EXPORTING NORTHERN PACIFIC LAND-GRANT TIMBER
WORSENS LOG SUPPLY CRISIS

Although the exportation of raw logs from federal and state forests in the Pacific Northwest is illegal, it is legal to export raw logs from lands held by individuals and corporations. This is true even for the formerly public forests whose current title derives from the 1864 and 1870 Northern Pacific railroad land grants.

Corporations sidestep log export prohibitions through a variety of substitution schemes. Regulations and laws banning raw log exports from federal lands do not prevent companies such as Plum Creek (a tax-free limited partnership) from exporting logs from railroad grant lands and using resulting profits to gain access to public timber — much of which is sold at a loss to the taxpayer.

Thus, the public's forests, which Congress gave to build and maintain a railroad, are converted via log exports to profits that are used to buy more public timber.

Log export docks in Longview, Washington, located along the Columbia River near Portland, Oregon.

Marianne Gordon

Checkerboard above Lake Kachess in the Cascade Range near Snoqualmie Pass, Washington state, August 1989.

Ron Reichel

Logs awaiting export. Ownership of many of the logs being exported overseas is based on Congress's Northern Pacific contracts — contracts that were repeatedly violated. Exported logs further exacerbate the forest crisis in the Pacific Northwest.

REFORMING THE 1864 LAND GRANT:
CONGRESS RETAINS OVERSIGHT AUTHORITY OF THE NORTHERN PACIFIC CONTRACTS.

Dictionary of American Portraits, Courtesy Library of Congress

President
Calvin Coolidge
(1872-1933)

Coolidge asked Congress for an investigation in 1924 after Northern Pacific threatened the National Forests.

President
Teddy Roosevelt
(1858-1919)

Roosevelt greatly expanded the National Forest System to keep the public forests out of the hands of timber syndicates. Despite this, timber corporations (many based on Congress's Northern Pacific contracts) have largely controlled National Forest policies and cut public trees, often at taxpayer expense.

Dictionary of American Portraits

IEPLC

"... Congress may, at any time, having due regard for the rights of said Northern Pacific Railroad Company, add to, alter, amend, or repeal this act."

— Section 20,
1864 Northern Pacific Railroad Land Grant

YIN AND YANG

AND

THE NORTHERN PACIFIC

Northern Pacific's trademark was the opposing forces of light (yang) and darkness (yin). Deriving from ancient Chinese philosophy, yin and yang represent opposing halves that comprise the whole. Northern Pacific used the symbol from 1893 until 1970, when Northern Pacific became Burlington Northern. (Yenne, 1991, p. 45.)

OVERCUTTING

N ASA satellite images comparing fragmented forests in the Pacific Northwest and the Amazon were published during the United Nation's Earth Summit in 1992 (see figures 2 and 3). Pacific Northwest forests were not always fragmented. The 1992 NASA satellite image of Pacific Northwest forests provides a startling contrast to the description of the region's forests in the early 1870s by Sam Wilkerson, Jay Cooke's publicist:

> The materials for the greatest lumber trade the world has seen exist on and near the Western end of this land grant, and maintain with a single interruption to the eastern foot of the Rocky Mountains. Forests . . . cover the larger part of Washington Territory, surpassing the woods of all the rest of the globe in the size, quality, and quantity of the timber. The firs in innumerable localities will cut 120,000 feet to the acre. Trees are common whose circumferences range from 20 to 50 feet, and whose heights vary from 200 to upward of 300 feet. The paradox of firs too large to be profitably cut into lumber, is to be seen all over Western Washington. . . . So prodigal is Nature in this region, and so wastefully fastidious is man, that lands yielding only 30,000 feet of

Figure 2. Forest Fragmentation – Amazon

[NASA/GSFC]

North of Manaus, Amazonas state, Brazil, 1990. As of 1992, about 11 percent of the Amazon Basin of Brazil had been deforested.

Figure 3. Forest Fragmentation – Pacific Northwest

Mt. Hood National Forest, Oregon, 1991. These satellite pictures demonstrate severe forest fragmentation in the Pacific Northwest as compared with the Amazon. About 10 percent of the native forest of the Pacific Northwest remains. Both of these NASA images were reprinted in the New York Times at the time of the United Nation's Earth Summit (Egan, June 11, 1992).

> lumber to the acre are considered to be hardly worth
> cutting over. . . .[179]

Although Wilkerson was generally given to hyperbole, the essence
of his assertions on the Pacific Northwest's native forests is correct.
Indeed, a 1923 Forest Service study, for example, revealed that the
states of Oregon, Washington, Idaho, Montana, and California held
over half the nation's remaining sawtimber.[180]

The forests of the Pacific Northwest retained their richness and
diversity until late into the 19th century. Since that time the forests
have become less rich and less diverse. One of the reasons for this
change has been the implementation of the 1864 and 1870 Northern
Pacific grants, when more than ten million acres of Northwestern
forests were claimed by the Northern Pacific Company.[181]

By 1890 Northern Pacific had begun to sell large blocks of the
grant lands to the syndicate run by Frederick Weyerhaeuser,
subsequently a neighbor of Northern Pacific magnate James J. Hill in
St. Paul, Minnesota. The Weyerhaeuser syndicate, much of whose
wealth was already based on the Northern Pacific grant lands, wielded
"practical control" over timber in Wisconsin and Minnesota.[182]

Weyerhaeuser shifted much of its operation to the Pacific
Northwest, and five years after Weyerhaeuser's first major purchase
of Northwestern grant lands from Northern Pacific in 1899, Washington
state became the nation's leading producer of timber. The geographical

---

[179]   Cited in Smalley, 1883, p.177.
[180]   U.S. Forest Service, 1923.
[181]   U.S. Bureau of Corporations, 1913-14, Part 1, pp.15-16; and Yenne,
1991, p.40.
[182]   *St. Paul Pioneer Press*, Jan. 3, 1900; and U.S. Bureau of Corporations,
1913-1914. In 1890 Frederick Weyerhaeuser and his partners Musser, Laird
Norton, and Denkmann bought 212,722 acres in eight Minnesota counties from
Northern Pacific for $452,330. The Pine Tree Lumber Company, one of the 49
companies owned or controlled by Weyerhaeuser and associates at this time, was
created. Pine Tree's debt was paid off by 1899, and over the next five years Pine
Tree paid 120 percent in dividends and cut 70 to 93 million board feet per year. By
1922 Pine Tree had paid stockholders - including Frederick Weyerhaeuser, who
controlled the company by holding 11 percent of the stock - $11.5 million. Despite
these profits, Pine Tree forfeited cutover lands to avoid paying taxes (Hidy, Hill,
and Nevins, 1963, pp.105-106,148-149,182,186).

shift on Weyerhaeuser's part was symbolic of the shift in the nation's center of timber production from the Midwest to the Pacific Northwest.

"Boil it all down to one sentence," said Franklin Roosevelt's Secretary of Agriculture Henry A. Wallace in 1940, "For over thirty years, beginning in 1905, Washington led the country in lumber cut, a dubious distinction that has now passed to Oregon."[183]

The Pacific Northwest's magnificent forests were largely cut over in an eight-decade industrial timber boom which is now nearing its end. It is not surprising, then, that large timber companies have recently shifted their capital and attention to the forests of the Southeast and of other parts of the world, notably Canada and, more recently, Siberia.[184] By 1991, the U.S. General Accounting Office reported that:

> The U.S. timber industry has shifted its center of gravity to an expanding area of plantations and secondary forests in the Southeast. By 1986, the southern states accounted for 47 percent of the nation's timber harvest, compared with 25 percent from the Pacific coast states. And the latter's share is expected to decline further.[185]

The liquidation of the region's forests has not gone unnoticed. Beginning in the 1980s, newspapers became increasingly interested in the controversy surrounding the overcutting of the region's forests. Headlines included:

Plum Creek Timber Co. Accused of Overcutting[186]

Logging Outstrips Growth[187]

Timber Companies Overcut Own Land, Eye Public Forests[188]

---

[183]   Wallace, 1940.
[184]   Strickland, 1992; and *Journal of Commerce*, Sept. 19, 1991.
[185]   U.S. General Accounting Office, 1991.
[186]   Sher, Sept. 22, 1986.
[187]   Manning, Oct. 16, 1988.
[188]   AP, Oct. 17, 1988.

Where Have All the Forests Gone?[189]

Private Timberlands Overcut, Officials Say[190]

Timber Firm Stirs Ire Felling Forests Faster Than They Regenerate[191]

Of Grants and Greed[192]

Government officials have publicly acknowledged the overcutting of the Pacific Northwest's forests. In 1990 Dan Evans, former Governor and U.S. Senator from Washington state, said, "We are seriously overcutting. The state's private forests are being cut at a rate faster than they can be regrown."[193] Former Washington state Lands Commissioner Brian Boyle stated that in response to corporate debt, the companies "go out and overcut to make the debt payments."[194]

Timber companies, too, are evidently aware of their own overcutting. According to a front page story in the *Wall Street Journal*, Plum Creek estimated the growth rate of trees on its railroad grant lands to be between 210 and 300 million board feet per year,[195] yet between 1984 and 1991 its annual cut from these lands averaged 605 million board feet.[196] The *Wall Street Journal* article quoted Bill Parson, Plum Creek's Rocky Mountain regional director, as saying, "We have never said we were on a sustained-yield program, and we have never been on a sustained-yield program. Let's get to the heart of it. Sure, it's extensively logged, but what is wrong with that?"[197]

Plum Creek is not alone. Consider Potlatch Corporation, whose land title also began with the Northern Pacific railroad grants. Jim Bates, former supervisor of the Clearwater National Forest, located

---

[189]   Egan, Feb. 15, 1989.

[190]   AP, April 14, 1990.

[191]   Farney, June 18, 1990.

[192]   Long, May 23, 1993.

[193]   UPI, 1990. Dan Evans soon became a director of Burlington Northern Railroad (Burlington Northern, 1991 Annual Report).

[194]   UPI, 1990.

[195]   Farney, June 18, 1990.

[196]   Plum Creek, May 1989; and Plum Creek, 1991 Annual Report.

[197]   Farney, June 18, 1990.

near extensive Potlatch holdings, was asked by a local county commissioner, "So they aren't operating on a sustained-yield basis, are they?" Bates' response was, "No, they are operating on a profit motive."[198]

Neil Sampson, executive vice president of the American Forestry Association wrote, "In some places, harvest levels have been unsustainable, the forest has been exploited, and the stewardship mandate has been violated."[199]

A former regional planning manager for Champion International, Jim Runyan, said, "If you look just at industry, you would say industry has overcut their lands, that they have removed their volumes too quickly, that they have created a hellacious hole or gap. I don't think anyone would disagree with that."[200]

Reports from Yellowstone Park to the Pacific Ocean indicate that this "hellacious hole" is felt across the entire region. What follows are some of these reports.

In Montana, the journalists Woodruff, Manning, and others have exposed the overcutting in that state. "The implications are fairly clear," Woodruff said, in quoting a Forest Service report. "Continuation of these levels of removals will eliminate the standing inventory volume on private lands in these counties in just a few decades."[201]

In north Idaho, Jeff Sher, a reporter with the *Spokesman-Review,* detailed Plum Creek's overcutting in north Idaho, quoting Avery District Ranger Crockett Dumas: "They're really going at it up there. We've got a serious concern." Sher also quoted Bob Boeh, Plum Creek's forest manager in north Idaho and eastern Washington: "We've determined it's in our best interests to harvest the timber as quickly as we can get into it and sell it, at least until we get out of this old growth backlog [sic]."[202]

Farther to the west, in the Colville region of eastern Washington, these problems were also evident. Sher quoted Harlan Young, county commissioner from Ione, Washington, saying of Plum Creek, "There's

---

[198]   *Lewiston Tribune,* Feb. 10, 1987.

[199]   Robertson, Nov. 22, 1990.

[200]   AP, Oct. 17, 1988. As indicated earlier, Champion sold 867,000 acres to Plum Creek in 1993 (*Seattle Times,* July 20, 1993; Dow Jones, Nov. 2, 1993).

[201]   Woodruff, Dec. 10, 1985. See also Manning, 1988 and 1989 articles.

[202]   Sher, Aug. 17, 1986.

considerable criticism that you guys are pretty insensitive to the continuing economy of the area, and the guys in the 25th story in downtown Seattle [Plum Creek headquarters], don't give a [expletive]."[203]

Moving west again, to the Snoqualmie Pass region of the Cascade Range, Timothy Egan of the *New York Times* reported the "shaving" of mountain sides around Roslyn, Washington. There, Plum Creek has extensively cut over the 155,000 acres of local land-grant forests. Peter Heide, Plum Creek's timberlands superintendent for the area, said that Plum Creek will leave no standing commercial timber for several generations. Company officials said that almost half of those trees are being exported to Japan, mostly in the form of raw logs,[204] thus bypassing local mills and jobs.

Along the Pacific Coast, Kim Severson and Elizabeth Moore of Tacoma's *Morning News Tribune* wrote of overcutting by domestic and foreign corporate raiders who have purchased hundreds of thousands of acres of forested lands for quick liquidation. In one example, two Asian corporations, Golden Springs International and TAT, bought from Weyerhaeuser 7,870 acres of land around Lake Roesiger, near Everett, Washington, and announced plans to log it all within two years to pay for the purchase. This rapid liquidation led to lawsuits by Snohomish County and was partially responsible for a strengthening of state regulation of private cutting.[205]

The *Oregonian* published a special report on October 15, 1990, entitled "Forests in Distress," which analyzed the conditions of the forests of the entire Pacific Northwest from Yellowstone National Park to the Pacific Ocean. This report provided an overview of region-wide damage to forests. In one article, "Private forests face critical log shortages," Forest Service economist Richard Haynes said private industry is simply running out of trees that are available to be cut.[206]

Yet some timber industry spokespeople have disputed the assertions of overcutting. Plum Creek's David Leland told journalist Dennis Farney of the *Wall Street Journal* that Plum Creek had to accelerate

---

[203] Sher, Sept. 22, 1986. Bowdlerism in the original.
[204] Egan, Feb. 15, 1989.
[205] Severson and Moore, May 27, 1990; and Dietrich, July 13, 1989.
[206] Durbin and Koberstein, Oct. 15, 1990.

its cut in 1982 and 1983 to get up to a sustained-yield cut.[207] This required, as he told Paul Koberstein of the *Oregonian*, the replacement of natural stands of old growth forest with tree plantations.[208] Similar arguments are forwarded by representatives of other timber companies. Weyerhaeuser, for example, claimed in a full-page advertisement in the *Seattle Times* and other papers that, "Our company manages its forests to provide a continuous flow of wood forever."[209]

Contrast Weyerhaeuser's assertion with statements such as that in the *Wall Street Journal*, "Weyerhaeuser is reaping big money from its trees as it saws wood as fast as it can," and from operators at its own sawmills, who say, "I don't know anybody in the country running harder than we are."[210]

Merely labeling current practices and rates of cutting as either sustainable or non-sustainable, however, is much less constructive than examining the effects of these practices on the forests and communities of the Pacific Northwest. And given its magnitude, Congress's 1864 Northern Pacific railroad land grant is clearly central to the unraveling of the fabric of the Pacific Northwest's forests and communities.

---

[207] Farney, June 18, 1990. But, as Farney wrote in the same article, "Mr. Leland's own figures indicate something far removed from sustained yield. Last year, he says, Plum Creek cut 597 million board feet; this year it targets about 500 million; in a few years it expects to throttle down to 450 million. Even the lowest figure, however, is well above his estimate of the annual growth rate of Plum Creek's forests: about 250 to 300 million board feet. Moreover, a Plum Creek prospectus last year [Plum Creek, May 1989] put the figure even lower: 'Approximately 210 million.' "

[208] Koberstein, Oct. 15, 1990, p.5.

[209] Weyerhaeuser, July 17, 1990.

[210] Weyerhaeuser employee Charles Moore, quoted by Bill Richards, 1992. Also, contrast Weyerhaeuser's statement with that of former U.S. Bureau of Land Management biologist Chris Maser: "No nation that I know of has maintained, on a sustainable basis, plantation managed trees beyond three rotations. The famous Black Forest in Europe is a plantation; it and other European forests are dying at the end of the third rotation. Nature's ancient forests are not renewable. The choice is ours, but the consequences belong to the generations of the future" (Maser, 1991, p.30).

ENVIRONMENTAL IMPACTS OF OVERCUTTING

This section summarizes some of the unintended yet inescapable impacts of current and historical levels of cutting on the Pacific Northwest's forests. It is not an exhaustive review of the scientific literature, and it does not address the question of relative worths of healthier versus less healthy forests. Further, while much of the recent research data on the impacts of logging on the condition of a forest derive from National Forest lands, it is clear that the effects are similar on the Northern Pacific grant forests.[211] Impact is usually measured by assessing effects on many of the components of forest ecosystems including watersheds, flora, and fauna.

Stream Sedimentation

Donald Potts, hydrologist and instructor at the University of Montana's Forestry School, stated, "I will say blatantly and outright that 99 percent of the sediment that enters water is the result of road construction and activity infringing too close to the riparian zones."[212]

Numerous studies have shown roads to be a highly significant source of erosion and consequent sedimentation of streams.[213]

Additional sedimentation occurs during or after logging: soil erodes when ground cover dies or is removed; skid trails turn up the soil and allow it to be washed away; bulldozers plow through streams. Former Forest Service hydrologist Allen Isaacson has stated that logging can be especially damaging in the headwaters of a stream, degrading channel stability all the way downstream.[214]

According to hydrologists Jon Rhodes of the Columbia River Inter-Tribal Fish Commission and Richard Jones of the Forest Service,

---

[211]   A healthy forest has been defined by Boyd E. Wickman, Chief Research Entomologist at the Forest Service's Forestry and Range Sciences Laboratory in La Grande, Oregon, as one where biotic and abiotic influences (e.g., insects, diseases, atmospheric deposition, silvicultural treatments, harvesting practices) do not threaten ecosystem stability for a given forest unit now or in the future (Wickman, 1992).

[212]   Manning, Oct. 19, 1988.

[213]   See, for example, Cederholm and Reid, 1987; Skille, 1991.

[214]   Isaacson, 1992.

the recovery of a watershed can take centuries. During this time road failures caused by heavy rains may continue to damage streams.[215]

Increased Water Yield

In the past few years, the Pacific Northwest has experienced floods resulting in human fatalities, blown-out streams, unraveling watersheds, and tens of millions of dollars in property damage; logging has been identified as a major exacerbating factor.[216]

Studies have shown that flooding and increased water yield are by-products of present and historical rates and methods of cutting.[217]

In addition, hillsides become highly susceptible to what are called "rain-on-snow" events, which occur when a warm moist Pacific maritime air mass moves into an area with snow on the ground. The combination of this common Pacific Northwest winter meteorological event with large logging-related openings in the forest canopy produces, according to Forest Service hydrologist Gary Kappesser, "higher flood peaks, shorter times to rise, and shorter recession. The result may be destabilized stream channels, with increased bedload transport."[218]

A striking example of the effects of rain-on-snow events can be seen in the heavily clearcut Coeur d'Alene River basin in north Idaho. There, Big Elk Creek, within a watershed which has been cut over, suffered a "200-year flood" on December 5, 1989, and another less than 40 days later. Contrast these floods with the floods that occurred simultaneously on Halsey Creek, which lies within a watershed with an intact forest canopy; these floods were only one-year and fifteen-year floods, respectively.[219]

Given the slow recovery rate for heavily-damaged watersheds, the deaths, environmental degradation, and millions of dollars in property damage from the winter floods of 1989-90 and 1990-91 may be harbingers of what the region's future flooding could bring.

---

[215]   Rhodes and Jones, 1991, p.9.
[216]   *New York Times*, 1990.
[217]   See for example, Heede, 1991; Rice, 1980; Christner and Harr, 1982.
[218]   Kappesser, 1991.
[219]   Kappesser, 1991.

Figure 4. Overcutting & Floods: Coeur d'Alene River Watershed North Idaho

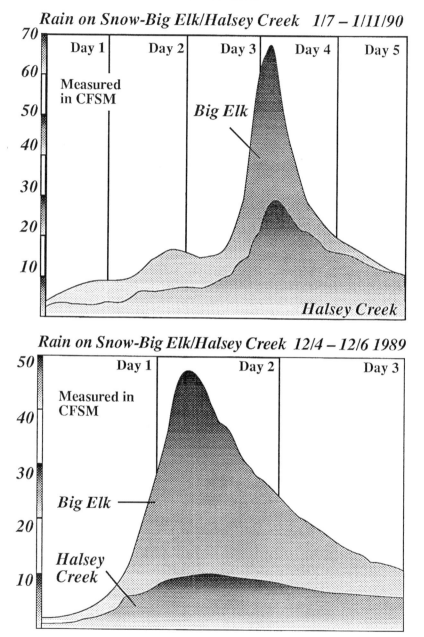

Comparison of stream flows from an extensively clearcut watershed (Big Elk Creek) with a watershed where the forest canopy has regrown and recovered hydrologically (Halsey Creek). Stream flows are expressed in units of cubic feet per square mile (cfsm) (adapted from Kappesser, 1991).

Damaged Fisheries

Overcutting has contributed to the decline of Pacific Northwest salmon stocks. The American Fisheries Society published a report in 1991 which identified 214 anadromous fish species in the Pacific Northwest that are at risk of extinction; the reasons include damage caused by logging, agriculture, and hydroelectric dams.[220] According to fisheries biologist Charles Frissell,

> . . . in many river basins of the Northwest where the number of threatened and endangered salmonid stocks is high, the most dramatic change in the landscape in recent decades has been extension of roads and clearcut logging into steep, erodible headwater areas. . . . [221]

Logging damages fish habitats and populations by increasing fine and bedload sediment, elevating water temperatures by decreasing shading of the water's surface, dramatically decreasing the number of pools, and by decreasing the large woody debris within the stream important for fish habitat.[222]

As hydrologists Jon Rhodes and Richard Jones wrote, "The severity and prevalence of these problems in fish habitat indicate that the past way of doing business is inadequate to protect water quality and fish habitat."[223]

Fragmentation

In the wake of worldwide concern over deforestation expressed at the 1992 Rio de Janeiro Earth Summit, NASA released satellite photos which, according to Dr. Compton Tucker, head scientist of the NASA project, clearly reveal the "tremendous degree of fragmentation" within the forests of the Pacific Northwest. Dr. Tucker stated that the forests of the Pacific Northwest are more fragmented than those of the

---

[220] Nehlson, Williams, and Lichatowich, 1991.
[221] Frissell, p.9.
[222] See, for example, Cederholm and Reid, 1987.
[223] Rhodes and Jones, 1991, p.2.

Amazon.[224] Former Chief of the Forest Service, Dale Robertson, joined timber company lobbyists in criticizing the photographs, saying, "You cannot see small trees from hundreds of miles in space."[225] Environmentalists countered that tree farms bear no resemblance to the old-growth interdependent forest communities they replace.[226] Further, while most of this region's forests used to be older than 300 years,[227] with a mix of species and ages, Weyerhaeuser now characterizes its plantation trees as varying only "from tiny seedlings to 60-year-old stands ready for harvest."[228]

Increased fragmentation means a reduction in the size of intact patches of forest. One clearly documented case is that of the Olympic National Forest in western Washington. In 1940 more than 87 percent of the old growth in the Olympic National Forest was in areas over 10,000 acres. By 1988 only one such patch (11,200 acres) remained. Sixty percent of the old growth remaining is in fragments smaller than 1,000 acres. Forty-one percent of the old growth is within 560 feet of an edge, eliminating its effectiveness as habitat for old growth interior-dwelling species. Trees on the edge also suffer greater mortality through blow-down.[229]

According to conservation biologist Reed Noss, fragmentation affects the native flora and fauna in various adverse ways. Many plants and animals which thrive in the interior of a forest are unable to survive elsewhere. Many animals will not cross clearings or roads, thus isolating local populations, making them less resilient to local catastrophes and more susceptible to local extinction. Small, isolated populations decrease genetic variation and gene flow, making the populations less adaptable. In addition, once a local population has been eliminated from a forest fragment, roads and clearings may inhibit other populations of the same species from reestablishing themselves.[230]

---

[224]   Egan, June 11, 1992.

[225]   AP, June 17, 1992.

[226]   AP, June 17, 1992.

[227]   Harris, 1984, p.11, citing early inventories by the U.S. Forest Service (1940) and the Pacific Northwest Loggers Association (1946).

[228]   Weyerhaeuser, July 24, 1990.

[229]   Morrison, 1990.

[230]   Noss, May 1992, p.2.

Damage to Native Plant and Wildlife Habitat

Multiple studies have assessed the damage that fragmentation inflicts on native species. The coordinator of the U.S. Fish and Wildlife Service's Grizzly Bear Recovery project, Chris Servheen, wrote, "Loss and fragmentation of natural habitat is particularly relevant to the management and survival of grizzly bears."[231] From Bob Summerfield, wildlife biologist for the U.S. Forest Service: "These [Southern Selkirk caribou] mortality sources are directly related to habitat security as influenced by human access into the habitat."[232] Forest Service biologists have reported that, "As road density increases to six miles per square mile, elk habitat use falls to zero."[233] Forest Service wildlife biologist L. Jack Lyon verified the strong negative correlation between road density and elk habitat quality.[234]

Biologists A.R. Weisbrod and W.D. Newmark each have documented the decline of large mammal species even within the protection of million-acre National Parks due to the fragmentation of surrounding habitat.[235] An in-depth analysis by the biologist Larry D. Harris on the effects of fragmentation of the Pacific Northwest forests cataloged declines of resident wildlife species.[236]

Further, increased fragmentation improves habitat for those species that are adapted to living in clearings or edges and allows these species to invade the habitats of forest-dwelling creatures. Industry officials commonly cite improved deer habitat, for example, as a reason for clearcutting, despite the fact that this sort of management favors opportunistic and globally common species and communities at the expense of rare and declining species and ecosystems. The populations of many forest-interior-dwelling neotropical songbirds are at risk from loss of habitat and invasion by such species as parasitic cowbirds. Many species of native plants are at risk of extinction from the proliferation of white-tailed deer caused by the clearing of forests. The

---

[231] Servheen, 1992, p.26.
[232] Summerfield, 1985, p.3.
[233] Wisdom, Bright, and Carey, 1986.
[234] Lyon, 1984.
[235] Weisbrod, 1976; and Newmark, 1985.
[236] Harris, 1984.

spotted owl is being displaced by the barred owl, a species not native to the western United States, because barred owls can make use of forests fragmented by clearcuts.[237]

Other species, such as the fisher, marten, and wolverine, retreat from areas which are fragmented. The wolverine has recently disappeared from Oregon's coastal range for exactly this reason.[238]

Regeneration and Soils

The accuracy of the data provided by the Forest Service concerning regeneration has come under question.[239] A report released in 1992 by the U.S. House of Representatives Interior Committee included an analysis suggesting that regrowth is only 64 percent of volume cut.[240]

The extent of successful regeneration on the grant lands is even less certain. While corporations have cut down most of the ancient forests on the grant lands, verifiable numbers on regeneration are unavailable.

Numerous factors suggest the difficulty of consistent regeneration on many cutover sites. One is the effect of logging on soil health. According to former U.S. Bureau of Land Management biologist Chris Maser, logging breaks the natural nutrient cycle, depriving the forest floor of natural nutrients, fungi, and both nitrogen-fixing bacteria and the species which inoculate the soil with them. These losses reduce soil health and thus forest health.[241]

Another factor limiting regeneration is the compaction of soils. It is generally accepted that the compaction of soils by heavy equipment used in logging can reduce the ability of the forest to regenerate.[242]

---

[237]   Noss, Dec. 1992; and Taylor and Forsman, 1976.
[238]   Noss, Dec. 1992.
[239]   See, for example, U.S. House Committee on Interior and Insular Affairs, 1992.
[240]   U.S. House Committee on Interior and Insular Affairs, 1992, p.2.
[241]   Maser, 1988.
[242]   See, for example, Adams.

Epidemics

Boll weevils taught cotton farmers the dangers of one-crop farming;[243] simplified systems have difficulty fending off species that feed on the system's remaining members.

The same holds true for simplified forest ecosystems. The habitat of predator species is often reduced through the simplification of the landscape. Fewer predators in many cases means more herbivorous insects – more "pests."

The simplification of forest ecosystems in the Pacific Northwest has encouraged regional outbreaks of spruce budworms, mountain pine beetles, and Douglas fir tussock moths, among others. As the Forest Service stated in its *Blue Mountains Forest Health Report*, "Scientific evidence suggests that we have encouraged conditions that may result in catastrophic levels of tree mortality."[244]

Numerous studies suggest that pathogens may be agents that help the forest return to a state of diversity and dynamic stability.[245] The Forest Service reported, also in its *Blue Mountains Forest Health Report*:

> . . . when human activities and processes fail to mimic the natural events that shape and define the vegetation conditions and character of stands, nature may intervene on its own behalf, through pest epidemics and catastrophic wildfires, to correct the unnatural state.[246]

---

[243]   The town of Enterprise, Alabama, put up a statue to the boll weevil because this insect destroyed the region's one-crop cotton farming and forced the region to diversify. Jim Young, technical editor to the magazine *Pulp and Paper,* suggested that the spotted owl also deserves such a monument, for forcing the communities of the Northwest to begin the process of diversification (cited in Robertson, Nov. 22, 1990).

[244]   Gast, Scott, and Schmitt, et al., 1991, p.1.

[245]   See, for example, Schowalter, 1991; Van der Kamp, 1991; and Noss, May, 1992.

[246]   Gast, Scott, and Schmitt, 1991.

Summary

The scientific literature shows that overcutting has been a major contributor to the ecological unraveling of forests in America's Pacific Northwest.

Clearly, the forests of the Pacific Northwest are in trouble. Watersheds are unraveling throughout the region. Vast areas of trees are susceptible to epidemics in the Blue Mountains of eastern Oregon and Washington. The spotted owl, the marbled murrelet, the grizzly bear, the gray wolf, many runs of salmon – these species have become threatened, endangered, or extinct.

Overcutting and tree-farming by the corporate heirs of Congress's Northern Pacific land grant have: (1) liquidated irreplaceable old growth throughout much of the region; (2) damaged streams such that many no longer sustain viable fish populations; (3) encouraged repeated catastrophic floods; (4) fragmented habitat to the extent that it is inadequate to support many indigenous forest species; (5) impoverished soils and the regenerative ability of forestlands; (6) encouraged the replacement of resilient natural communities with highly vulnerable monocrops; (7) liquidated forests which have sustained healthy populations of flora and fauna; and (8) superimposed artificial "checkerboards" of clearcuts within the National Forests.

These Northern Pacific checkerboards are the next subject of this discussion.

THE CHECKERBOARDS

A casual glance at maps of the Pacific Northwest reveals a pattern of mixed land ownership in the National Forests. Federal lands alternate, often by the square mile, with lands claimed by corporations. Many of the corporate claims in the Pacific Northwest originated in the 1864 and 1870 Northern Pacific land grants.

These square-mile checkerboards were drawn to the specifications of ease and economics, not biology. Artificial boundaries mean nothing to the trees, fish, grizzly bear, elk, and deer that live within the forest. Streams cross and recross ownership boundaries, carrying within them silt from roads and logging operations.

The problems are exacerbated by the sheer number of checkerboards: the Gallatin National Forest, for example, has within its borders 1.7 million acres of private or corporate checkerboards, most of which derive from the Northern Pacific grants.[247] Plum Creek claims 2.1 million acres, many of which were in checkerboards; Weyerhaeuser controls checkerboard lands, as do Boise Cascade, Potlatch, and other major timber companies. Each square mile of corporate checkerboard influences the four square miles adjacent to it, and, clearly, each square mile of National Forest land can be immediately affected by up to four sections of railroad grant lands. Just as clearly, within many of the National Forests of the region, the management philosophies alternate by the square mile.

Problems with the checkerboards were recognized by Franklin Roosevelt's Secretary of Agriculture, Henry A. Wallace. In 1940 he wrote:

> Sound management of the national forests, including their wise use in such a way as to stabilize the forest situation in the public interest, is further handicapped by large interior private holdings. . . . Too often these are key tracts which hamstring both national forest administration and beneficial public influence on practices followed on private lands.[248]

Today the checkerboards remain, and accelerated cuts on privately claimed sections make the concerns more pressing than ever.

The Forest Service has many times been forced to reduce its cut in attempts to compensate for corporate overcutting on adjacent checkerboards. Orville Daniels, supervisor of the Lolo National Forest, announced a cut reduction in 1991. In a "Dear Concerned Citizen" letter dated September 22, 1991, Daniels gave reasons for the reduction. First among them was that:

> . . . the rate of logging has been higher than we anticipated on about 400,000 acres of privately owned forested lands within the boundaries of the Lolo. The

---

[247] Williams, James M., 1989.
[248] Wallace, 1940.

cumulative effects of both private cutting at the current rate and Lolo cutting at the planned rate would violate resource protection standards for wildlife cover and watershed buffering. The result is a significant reduction in harvest [sic] on 289,000 "suitable" acres.[249]

The decision to reduce the cut was labeled as "premature" by then Forest Service Chief Dale Robertson[250] and as "arrogant" by lobbyists for the timber companies.[251]

A second well-documented example of how corporate cutting on checkerboard lands increases the difficulty of National Forest management took place in the Avery District of the Idaho Panhandle National Forests (IPNF). A review of the planning files on the IPNF reveals a series of documents and memoranda that underscore the problem of the railroad checkerboard and management of the National Forests. In 1979 the Avery District Ranger requested that the Forest Service address problems of checkerboard land ownership in its forest plan.[252] The Forest Service failed to do so. Later, Burlington Northern[253] declined to provide the ranger district personnel with information regarding Burlington Northern's management plans for the railroad checkerboard lands, thus removing the possibility of "mutual participation" in the planning process.[254]

In 1982 the Avery District Ranger urged a reduction in cut to allow for increased impacts from private cutting.[255] Finally, an internal analysis, called the "Yellow Paper," listed effects of Burlington Northern liquidation of trees on that part of the IPNF.[256] These included: reduced fisheries, insufficient elk cover, reduced visual quality, clearcuts exceeding 40 acres in size, and the loss of the old-growth "component." Again, these concerns were disregarded, and

---

[249]   Daniels, Sept. 22, 1991.

[250]   Devlin, Sept. 17, 1991.

[251]   Devlin, Sept. 13, 1991.

[252]   U.S. Forest Service IPNF Planning Document 0882.

[253]   This Forest Plan was written before Plum Creek was spun off, so the grant lands were at this time controlled by Burlington Northern.

[254]   U.S. Forest Service IPNF Planning Document 0892.

[255]   U.S. Forest Service IPNF Planning Document 1775.

[256]   U.S. Forest Service IPNF Planning Document 1710.

the District was ultimately assigned a cut nearly twice the level recommended by the local ranger.[257]

On some National Forests, the Forest Service has simply ignored the cumulative environmental effects of Burlington Northern's accelerated logging. Planning files for the Colville National Forest in northeastern Washington state are largely silent on this cumulative effects issue.[258]

Management of the National Forests is made more difficult by the construction of roads for access to privately claimed sections of the checkerboard. This access extends even into wilderness study areas. Plum Creek built roads into the Gallatin Mountain Range wilderness study area in the 1980s. U.S. Representative Pat Williams (D-MT) attempted to block these roads, saying, "I'm very disappointed at BN's[259] action in building the road. The question isn't whether it's a legal road – it is – but it's the first step toward logging of three sections in the middle of the whole area."[260]

The legality of such roads has been questioned. The legality is based on what is called the "Melcher Language," after the U.S. Senator who inserted language into the 1980 Alaska Lands Act guaranteeing that inholders within wilderness study areas would have access to their claims. Some contend that the Melcher Amendment applies only to lands in Alaska.[261]

Examples abound of the difficulties presented by roads crossing Forest Service lands to the checkerboards. In the Clearwater National Forest in Idaho, Plum Creek asked for permission to build two miles of roads through the National Forest in order to reach some of its claimed inholdings. Finding that these roads would have significantly damaged the watershed, the District Ranger denied this access,

---

[257] The District Ranger suggested targets of 22.68 million board feet per year for the first ten years and 17.63 million board feet per year thereafter (U.S. Forest Service IPNF Planning Document 1699). The District was assigned 40 million board feet per year, with an additional five million board feet per year for pulp and salvage (U.S. Forest Service IPNF Planning Document 1690, titled "IPNF Final Plan Development," May 2, 1986).

[258] John Osborn, hearing record of the oral presentation, appended statement pp.9-11, Colville National Forest Plan Appeal No. 3163, Dec. 21, 1990.

[259] Burlington Northern, Plum Creek's corporate parent.

[260] AP, Sept. 13, 1987.

[261] Jones, Dec. 5, 1981.

instead allowing the company to build 100 yards of road elsewhere to reach this same property. Plum Creek appealed the decision, charging it increased Plum Creek's costs and thus amounted to an illegal "taking."[262] In the Idaho Panhandle National Forests, the Forest Service recently decided to allow Plum Creek to build roads which cross the headwaters of the East Fork of Bluff Creek 51 times.[263]

The checkerboard legacy of the railroad grant renders impossible a coherent management strategy. Market-driven corporate strategies alternate by the square mile with national conservation commitments to sustaining forest ecosystems. It is not unusual to see genetic islands of standing forest fragments surrounded by miles of stumps. Until the problems of the checkerboard inholdings are resolved, the goal of ecosystem management and sustainable forestry within the National Forests will remain unreachable.

SQUEEZE ON TIMBER SUPPLY

Most credible studies by the U.S. Forest Service, state forestry departments, and academic analysts indicate there will be a shortfall of timber supply on corporate timberland in the near future, and that this will increase pressure to further overcut the National Forests. As this section will show, this shortage is in line with the history of the timber industry: big timber corporations have historically overcut region, and then moved on. Further, this section will show that a handful of major companies control a majority of the region's total milling capacity as well as timberland. It will also investigate the effects that the overcutting of corporate controlled lands has on the National Forests and on the U.S. Forest Service. It will show that increased cutting on public lands cannot make up for the shortage caused by timber industry overcutting. And finally, it will suggest that any solution to either the environmental or employment problems

---

[262] Loftus, Jan. 4, 1992. The Forest Service's counter-offer would have required the corporation to use helicopter- and longline skyline-logging to pull out the trees.

[263] July 1, 1992. U. S. Forest service decision notice and accompanying environmental assessment approving the Fortune in Bathtubs Special Use Access Permit for Plum Creek Timber Company.

must relate to the handful of corporations which control much of the region's timberland and milling capacity.

Shortfall of Timber Supply

In 1963 the Forest Service published the study, *Timber Trends in Western Oregon and Western Washington*, which concluded that if then-current management trends and policies continued, annual rates of cutting could not be sustained and would decline near the end of the century.[264] The study foretold supply shortages as the last of the old-growth forests were cut, followed two or three decades later by a return to historic levels of cutting as second growth trees became large enough to cut. In 1992 Sample and LeMaster of the American Forestry Association commented on the inevitability of this transition:

> *Whether* there would be a timber supply decline and subsequent contraction within the forest products industry was never in question, it was simply a matter of *when,* by how much, and for how long the industry would contract before beginning to expand again as more second-growth timber reached harvestable size.[265]

In 1987, *A Report on Idaho's Timber Supply*, compiled by the Forest Service at the direction of the Reagan Administration, concluded, among other things, that north Idaho had enough trees to allow cutting to continue for another ten years, depending on how quickly the trees were cut on corporate lands. Echoing the 1963 report, the 1987 report also stated, "In subsequent years, however, a significant decline in harvest levels from these [corporate lands] is inevitable."[266]

According to a 1987 study, U.S. Forest Service, Montana state, and university researchers do not believe there are enough trees in Montana to supply all mills, regardless of the level at which the Forest Service sets its allowable cut. They have written that, "[T]he full mill capacity level cannot be met over the entire projection period [of 1985

---

264   U.S. Forest Service, 1963.
265   Sample and LeMaster, 1992, p.5; emphasis in the original.
266   LeVere, Raettig, and Green, 1987.

to the year 2030] because there simply is not enough timber inventory."[267]

Similarly, as of 1991, large trees (trees over 100 years old) cover less than a quarter of non-National Forest land in western and northwestern Montana, according to U.S. Forest Service Resource Bulletins. Nonstocked and poorly to medium-stocked stands occupy nearly two-thirds of timberland areas outside National Forests.[268]

The lack of trees – not merely legal constraints – will cause the shortfall in Montana. In the year 2005, "[H]arvest level drops below the full mill capacity processing level because [the] needed level of harvesting cannot be physically met. . . ."[269]

The large corporations in Montana have overcut; in comparison, other timberland ownerships (public and non-timber industry) are relatively well-off. According to the 1987 analysis of the Montana timber supply, the "forest industry's cut falls sharply at [the year] 2000 while other ownerships maintain a constant harvest. Industry's harvest decrease is a significant event. . . . This results from inadequate inventory and is the major cause of the statewide harvest decline. . . ."[270]

A U.S. Forest Service survey of Montana's forests in 1985 reached similar conclusions about pending shortfalls:

> Over 70 percent of the roundwood removals [timber cut] came from four counties in northwestern Montana (Lincoln, Flathead, Sanders, and Missoula). In these counties, the removals from lands owned by forest industry far exceeded growth. . . . The implications are fairly clear: continuation of these levels of removals will eliminate the standing inventory volume on private lands in these counties in just a few decades. . . . Present demands on public forests and commitments for future generations make it questionable whether these lands can or will make up the entire difference.[271]

---

267   Flowers, Bricknell, Green, et al, 1987, p.7.
268   Collins and Conner, 1991, p.7; O'Brien and Conner, 1991, p.6.
269   Flowers, Bricknell, Green, et al, 1987, p.8.
270   Flowers, Bricknell, Green, et al, 1987, p.10.
271   Green, O'Brien, and Schaefer, 1985, p.27.

The public forests simply cannot make up the shortfall caused by corporate overcutting. "Increases in harvest on National Forest lands . . . are not large enough to offset the decrease in harvest by the industrial ownerships."[272] While this study referred directly to western Montana, the conclusions are likely applicable wherever the corporations have overcut.

The Natural History of the Timber Industry

Corporate spokespeople sometimes acknowledge that the region is undergoing a historic transition. George Weyerhaeuser, great-grandson of Frederick Weyerhaeuser and current chairman of Weyerhaeuser's board of directors, told a gathering of company employees in 1991, "[T]he competitive environment within the forest products industry has changed dramatically and permanently since 1980."[273] Magazines associated with the timber trade, such as *Forest Industries*, *Pulp and Paper*, and *American Forests,* have editorialized that the timber industry is not facing up to the changes which are occurring.[274]

The natural history of this industry has been for corporations to cut over a region and then move on. The timber industry's flight from New England prompted George Perkins Marsh to write his seminal book, *Man and Nature*, in 1864, ironically the same year as the original Northern Pacific grant.[275] Ten years later, Dr. Franklin Hough, moved by Marsh's writings and by the destruction of the forests in the Great Lakes region, urged Congress to protect its remaining forests.[276]

---

[272]   Flowers, Bricknell, Green, et al, 1987, p.18.

[273]   Blumenthal, Aug. 18, 1991. It is important to note that this speech was made *prior* to the spotted owl's listing under the Endangered Species Act, and also that recent court injunctions halting timber sales have been based not on the Endangered Species Act, but on two other pieces of federal legislation, the National Forest Management Act and the National Environmental Policy Act.

[274]   Robertson, Nov. 22, 1990.

[275]   Marsh, 1864.

[276]   Hough, 1874. Dr. Hough's work helped create the U. S. Forest Service and prepare the ground for the creation of the National Forest System (Hough, 1878-1884).

By 1905 the timber industry had shifted from the Great Lakes to the vast old growth forests of the Pacific Northwest. In 1940 Franklin Roosevelt's Secretary of Agriculture Henry Wallace addressed the Northwest about its timber future in a letter to the *Seattle Post-Intelligencer*:

> [M]any private owners have followed and still do follow the cut-out and get-out philosophy. . . . [C]arried to its conclusions, the philosophy will pauperize a region.
> Under the extreme form of this philosophy, holdings are built up solely for the maximum returns from the virgin timber. Ownership shifts rapidly, is characteristically unstable, and forms exceedingly complex patterns. . . .
> . . . The resource back of community after community is being liquidated. Forest industries are disappearing. Each disappearance is a solar plexus blow to the community, to the region. The Grays Harbor, Puget Sound, Lower Columbia, Klamath County and Deschutes districts in your region are headed directly toward trouble that hit Pennsylvania, the Lake States, and the Missouri Ozarks. Those areas were successively cut out and left stranded for generations while a new crop took time to grow. While your region has gone far down the wrong road, it can yet turn back.[277]

This warning, directed specifically towards the Pacific Northwest, came five years after Ferdinand A. Silcox, the U.S. Forest Service's Chief Forester, had addressed the annual meeting of the Society of American Foresters in 1935, saying:

> The forests of the country must regain and hold permanently their place as sources of employment in every forest region. They must become centers around which communities may be assured a stable existence. Human welfare, opportunities for useful employment,

---

[277] Wallace, Aug. 25, 1940. In many of the areas mentioned by Wallace, a major force in the timber industry was Weyerhaeuser.

permanent communities, and all the other social benefits that flow from productive forests must be our goal. In the past, we have laid much stress on forestry for timber production, without much regard to its immediate benefit to the surrounding communities. The lumber industry was concerned merely with the extraction of logs for the immediate profit that might be made, and gave little or no consideration to the social consequences of timber depletion.[278]

Speaking before the National Control Committee of the Lumber Code Authority two months later, Silcox said:

In frankness I must say, however, that as far as I can see after traveling widely over this Country, a large portion of the lumber industry is still operating on the basis of quick liquidation, draining off the new remaining reservoirs of virgin timber, with the usual inevitable result.[279]

The timber industry was quick to belittle these charges. Lumberman Henry F. Chaney objected to what he called "the old theme of abandoned lumber and sawmill towns," arguing that by their very nature timber communities were "never considered anything but tools in the rescuing of the timber [sic] and would be discarded just like a worn-out hoe or plow or any other piece of equipment whose purpose had been served." He continued, "Outside the rescuing a timber body [sic] in some pestilential swamp in Louisiana or pine flat in Wisconsin or Michigan, what other purpose would be served by maintaining a town there?"[280]

Timber corporations today face accusations of overcutting the Pacific Northwest's forests and moving on. Forest Service economist Richard Haynes said in 1990 that private industry has created a supply problem which our grandchildren will inherit. Asked about industry's response to the shortage, he responded, "You'll probably see all of the big companies leave the region."[281]

---

[278] Quoted in Twining, 1985, p.135.
[279] Twining, 1985, 136.
[280] Twining, 1985, p.135.
[281] Durbin and Koberstein, Oct. 15, 1990.

This is already happening. Anderson and Olson tracked the flight of lumber and plywood capacities from the Pacific Northwest[282] between 1978 and 1990. As Figure 5 demonstrates, the major companies are reducing their mill capacities in the Northwest and increasing their capacities in the Southeast.[283]

Figure 5. Percent Changes in Lumber and Plywood Capacity

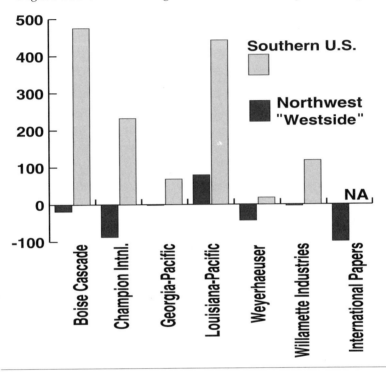

---

[282]   Note that this is for western Washington and western Oregon, and does not include the "Inland Empire." The Inland Empire consists roughly of western Montana, northern Idaho, eastern Washington, and eastern Oregon.

[283]   Our source for Figure 5 and the following data is Anderson and Olson, 1991, p.43.

Percent change in lumber and plywood capacity:

Company	Northwest "Westside"	Southern U.S.
Boise Cascade	-19	+475
Champion Intnl.	-88	+232
Georgia-Pacific	-2	+68
Louisiana-Pacific	+79	+442
Weyerhaeuser	-44	+18
Willamette Industries	-4	+118
Intnl. Paper	-100	NA
Regionwide change	-34	+121

The timber frontier has moved from Maine to Pennsylvania, from Pennsylvania to the Great Lakes, from the Great Lakes to the Southeast and to the Pacific Northwest. Now the frontier is on the move again. Weyerhaeuser, Boise Cascade, and others have their sights set on Siberia.[284] Weyerhaeuser, Boise Cascade, Champion, and Louisiana-Pacific are moving back to the Southeast. As Jude White of International Paper said to the forester Gordon Robinson, "Hell, Robbie. We're on sustained yield. When we clean up the timber in the West, we'll return to New England, where the industry began."[285]

Unlike the nineteenth century lumberjacks who followed the timber corporations westward, timber workers today are left behind as corporations shift their capital. Independent loggers and local millowners are forced into competition for the trees that remain after the big companies have finished cutting. Many leave the industry. This is already happening in Montana, according to the University of Montana's Bureau of Business and Economic Research. Between 1981 and 1989, the number of mills declined from 142 to 87 (a reduction of 39 percent). The greatest decline occurred in small mills (those with capacities less than ten million board feet per year), from 114 to 58, a reduction of 49 percent.[286]

Significantly, there has been a concurrent concentration of power among those mills which remain. The same University of Montana study revealed that the number of mills with capacities of greater than 50 million board feet increased from five to 13.[287] Other studies have revealed that in 1981 the 13 largest mills in Montana produced 70 percent of the lumber,[288] and the largest 28 produced 93 percent of the lumber.[289]

Similar trends are true in Northwestern states other than Montana. In 1979 the 14 largest of the 133 mills in Idaho produced 49 percent

---

[284] *Journal of Commerce*, Sept. 19, 1991; *Spokesman-Review*, June 26, 1992; and Gregory Wright, June 22, 1990.

[285] Robinson, 1988, p.18. Robinson was formerly a forester for Southern Pacific.

[286] Keegan, Swanson, Wichman, and Van Hooser, 1990, p.12.

[287] Keegan, Swanson, Wichman, and Van Hooser, 1990, p.12.

[288] Keegan, Jackson, and Johnson, 1983, p.11.

[289] Green, O'Brien, and Schaefer, 1985, p.29.

of the total lumber.[290] In 1985 eight mills processed 28 percent of Idaho's total.[291]

Large corporations control an inordinate amount of the total milling capacity. In the early 1990s, the largest four timber companies in the Inland Empire[292] (Louisiana-Pacific, Potlatch, Boise Cascade, and Plum Creek) controlled more than a third of the total production.[293] The largest ten corporations control more than half of the region's capacity.[294] Plum Creek's mill capacity is over 400 million board feet per year, while the average annual amount of timber sold in Forest Service Region One (generally Montana and north Idaho) during the 10 year period from 1984 to 1993 was 786 million board feet.[295]

Plum Creek claims 1.54 million of the 1.7 million acres (90 percent) of industrial timber land in Montana.[296]

This sort of market share, and this sort of control, makes each of the big four companies likely to be, as an executive of Plum Creek has said, "a survivor of the crunch that will occur in the industry."[297]

---

[290]   Keegan, Jackson, and Johnson, 1982, p.14.

[291]   Keegan, Martin, Johnson, and Van Hooser, 1988, p.62. That is, 410 million of the total 1.452 billion board feet.

[292]   Montana, Idaho, eastern Washington, and eastern Oregon.

[293]   The calculations are based on data from the American Plywood Association (APA, 1991); the Directory of the Forest Products Industry (DFPI, 1992); and the Western Wood Products Association (WWPA, 1992, pp.22-23). Most of the data from the WWPA are actual production figures for the year 1990. Plywood data from the APA were converted using 2.57 square feet (3/8 inch) plywood for each board foot, as suggested by Keegan, Martin, Johnson, and Van Hooser, 1988, p.63. Our calculations showed five companies, but the 1993 sale of Champion's lands in Montana to Plum Creek removed Champion from the list.

[294]   DFPI, 1992; and WWPA, 1992; and APA, 1991. The ten were the above four plus Champion, DAW, W-I, WTD, Idaho Forest Industries, and Vaagen. Much of Champion's, DAW's and W-I's production has since been acquired by Stimson and Crown Pacific. See both 1993 articles by Schwennesen.

These figures understate the amount of control by the major companies. The familial, historical, and business connections between Potlatch and Boise Cascade must be kept in mind. There are, in addition, other mills with ties to the big four. For example, the president of Idaho Forest Industries is the twin brother of the president of Potlatch.

[295]   Plum Creek, 1991 Annual Report; and Warren, 1994, p.120.

[296]   Calculated from Plum Creek, 1988; Dow Jones, Aug. 5, 1992; and Dow Jones, Nov. 2, 1993; and Waddell, et al, 1989, p.23.

[297]   Woodruff, 1989.

Significantly, these are precisely the corporations large enough to relocate, and (with the exception of Louisiana-Pacific) these are precisely the corporations based largely on Congress's Northern Pacific railroad land grants.

Pressure to Overcut the National Forests

The response to these difficulties by many mill owners as well as many politicians has been to pressure the Forest Service for higher cut levels, thereby further postponing and increasing the precipitousness of the inevitable and long-predicted transition. Bob Anez of the Associated Press wrote that representatives of both Champion and Plum Creek approached Montana's governor and "suggested the administration could intercede with the U.S. Forest Service to persuade the federal agency to make more land available."[298] The interference by politicians such as then-U.S. Senator Jim McClure (R-ID) in the management of the National Forests is well documented.[299] McClure, who within weeks of retiring from the Senate became a director of Boise Cascade,[300] has been quoted as saying about Forest Service planning, "And if you just jiggle a few numbers in [the Forest Service] computer you can come up with the higher harvest."[301] Such interference has inflated National Forest timber targets, raised unrealistic expectations on the part of workers, and escalated conflict over shrinking forests between corporate lobbyists, politicians, and upper-level Forest Service managers on one hand and Forest Service scientists and conservationists on the other.

One outcome of this interference, and of the Forest Service's attempts to shore up timber supplies by overcutting the public forests,

---

[298]   Anez, Aug. 15, 1989.
[299]   See, for example, McCarthy, 1986; or *Lewiston Tribune*, Sept. 25, 1987. See also James McClure's Sept. 17, 1987 letter to Forest Service Chief Dale Robertson (reprinted in *Transitions*, Oct. 1988, pp.3-5). For examples of intercession on behalf of the timber industry by other politicians, see Conrad Burns' Sept. 10, 1990 letter (reprinted in *Transitions*, Dec. 1991, p. 11) and Larry Craig's May 23, 1991 letter (reprinted in *Transitions*, Aug. 1991, p. 8), both to Robertson.
[300]   AP, Dec. 14, 1990. More recently, McClure has lobbied Congress on behalf of Potlatch Corporation (Dean Miller, Sept. 25, 1994).
[301]   *Lewiston Tribune*, Oct. 31, 1988.

has been the collapse of the Forest Service's credibility as a professional agency.

Forest Service use of inaccurate data to support unsustainable levels of cutting and reforestation failures on the National Forests were substantiated in a U.S. House Interior Committee investigation.[302] Former Committee Chair George Miller (D-CA) said on release of the Committee's report, "This report shows that in spite of repeated reassurances by the Forest Service, the forests we've cut down are not growing back. . . . The mismanagement of these forests has been devastating."[303]

Many within the agency have recognized that the Forest Service cannot for long meet industry-driven timber targets. In 1990 supervisors from 63 National Forests sent a pair of memos to former Forest Service Chief Dale Robertson which warned that the agency was "out of control." The supervisors said too much of the National Forest budget went to timber sales and not enough to recreation, fish and wildlife enhancement, and soil and water protection."[304] The Association of Forest Service Employees for Environmental Ethics has been formed in response to problems within the agency and Forest Service intransigency to attempts at reform from within.

While former Forest Service Chief Robertson said in an interview that the internal debate was good for the Forest Service,[305] the response by top Forest Service officials has been to silence many scientists and other agency professionals whose findings conflicted with logging plans. For example, Thomas Lake, a 25-year Forest Service wildlife specialist in California, was told in a letter from his supervisor that "any outside activity that may tend to bring criticism of, or embarrassment to, the Forest Service, is forbidden."[306] This is not a unique occurrence: Francis Mangels, a Forest Service biologist, has said that a district ranger falsified his scientific reports; Landon Smith, a Forest Service archeologist, was banned from the field and assigned computer work when he complained about logging damage to archeological sites.[307]

---

[302]   U.S. House Committee Staff, 1992.
[303]   Sonner, June 16, 1992.
[304]   Durbin, Jan. 7, 1990.
[305]   Egan, March 4, 1990.
[306]   Sonner, Sept. 8, 1991.
[307]   Sonner, Sept. 8, 1991.

Corporate pressure, including that from the Congress's land-grant-based timber corporations, was behind the forced retirement of Regional Forester John Mumma, who failed to meet politically driven timber targets in Region 1.[308] Mumma testified before Congress that he failed to meet these targets because to do so would have forced him to violate federal laws. He also said, "Over the past years, I have experienced several instances of what I regard as undue interference and pressure by political figures. . . . I believe that this interference was designed to force me to make decisions unwarranted by existing law."[309] These are only a few of the documented cases.

Congress and the American people have been warned repeatedly that the *modus operandi* of the timber industry is to liquidate the forests of a region and then move on to cut over new forests elsewhere. In the Pacific Northwest the overcutting has been facilitated by the concentration of immense tracts of forested land, with the wealth and power that comes with them, into the hands of a very few timber companies, whose wealth derives from the 1864 and 1870 Northern Pacific land grants. These companies have systematically liquidated their own forests, and then have used their considerable political and economic power to gain access to the public's forests.

The overcutting of the forests of the Pacific Northwest by Congress's land-grant-based timber corporations, with resultant damage to the ecological and economic health of the region, raises two questions: Has the public been well served by Congress's 1864 and 1870 Northern Pacific grants? Has the public interest been protected by Congress, the institution that retains oversight authority of the Northern Pacific contracts?

---

[308]   Mostly north Idaho and western Montana.
[309]   Loftus, May 8, 1992.

Log Exports

Tightening the Timber Supply Squeeze

Despite a widely acknowledged timber squeeze in the Pacific Northwest, about one of every four trees cut in Oregon and Washington are exported unprocessed to Japan, China, and Korea; since 1988, U.S. log exports have been worth more than $2 billion every year.[310] As Tom Mayr, of the Mayr Brothers lumber mill in Hoquiam, Washington, has said, "If a log is of export quality, and is available to be exported, it will be exported. It will not be available to a domestic mill."[311]

Since 1990 the exportation of raw logs from federal and state forests in the Pacific Northwest has been illegal; however, it *is* legal to export raw logs from lands titled to individuals and corporations. This is true even for the formerly public forests whose current titles derive from the 1864 and 1870 Northern Pacific land grants.

It is widely held that the reduction of log exports is key to expanding the Pacific Northwest timber supply.[312] In designating critical habitat for the spotted owl, the U.S. Fish and Wildlife Service stated that shortfalls from protecting the spotted owl could be made up by a small reduction in log exports.[313] A federal ban of "private" log

---

[310]   Miller, 1991, p.204.

[311]   Klahn, May 31, 1989.

[312]   Anderson and Olson, 1991; and U.S. Fish and Wildlife Service, 1991-1992.

[313]   U.S. Fish and Wildlife Service, 1991-1992.

exports could possibly provide an additional three billion board feet a year for domestic processing.[314]

Until the early 1960s, raw log exports were a small factor in the timber economy. Since that time raw log exports from the West Coast have increased dramatically. Figure 6 shows this overall increase between 1961 and 1992.

Figure 6. Raw Log Exports from the West Coast[315]

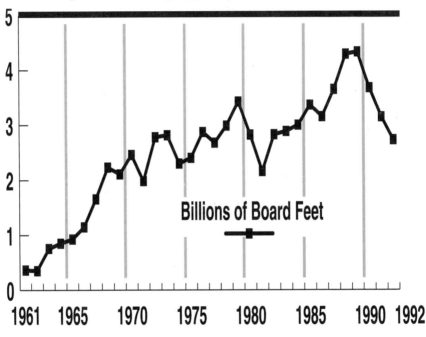

---

[314]   Anderson and Olson, 1991, p.76; and Thomas, 1989.

[315]   Ulrich, 1988, p.26; and Warren, 1991, pp.24,30,32; and Warren, 1992, pp.1,32,34; and Western Wood Products Association, *Statistical Yearbooks of the Western Lumber Industry*, 1973, 1983, and 1992. Figure 6 includes exports from California and Alaska. The volume of logs in billion board feet from 1961 to 1992 is as follows:

1961	0.364;	1962	0.351;	1963	0.756;	1964	0.852;
1965	0.927;	1966	1.147;	1967	1.654;	1968	2.233;
1969	2.109;	1970	2.460;	1971	1.982;	1972	2.780;
1973	2.816;	1974	2.302;	1975	2.405;	1976	2.873;
1977	2.679;	1978	2.988;	1979	3.428;	1980	2.824;
1981	2.162;	1982	2.828;	1983	2.887;	1984	3.001;
1985	3.366;	1986	3.153;	1987	3.653;	1988	4.292;
1989	4.331;	1990	3.681;	1991	3.148;	1992	2.732.

THE EXPORTATION OF RAW LOGS FROM CONGRESS'S GRANT LANDS

As described earlier, the two largest current holders of Northern Pacific grant lands are Plum Creek and Weyerhaeuser.

Plum Creek

Plum Creek has divided itself into the Cascade Region (east and west slopes) and the Rocky Mountain Region (northeastern Washington, Idaho, and Montana). In 1989 Plum Creek exported 59 percent of its Cascade cut. This declined to 55 percent in 1990 and 43 percent in 1991,[316] primarily because Plum Creek is receiving higher prices locally. The 1990 raw log exports, 100 million board feet, primarily of old growth, accounted for 20 percent of Plum Creek's total cut from both regions.[317] In 1992 sixteen percent of Plum Creek's log volume went to Asia.[318]

Plum Creek (and others) also export trees which have been minimally processed. Canted logs (squared so they stack more easily) are counted as "processed" rather than raw; chipped logs (for pulpwood) and flitched logs (a cant with two round sides) are also counted as "processed." Neither operation adds much value or generates significant employment.

Weyerhaeuser

Weyerhaeuser exports one of every three logs cut from the Pacific Northwest lands it controls. In 1991 this amounted to 500 million board feet of second growth trees,[319] 90 percent of which originated from Washington state, the rest being exported from Oregon.[320] Weyerhaeuser and 30 other companies (including Boise Cascade) filed notices with the U.S. Forest Service that they would cut back

---

[316] Plum Creek, 1991 Form 10-K, p.1-2.
[317] Plum Creek, 1990 Annual Report, p.4.
[318] Plum Creek, 1992 Annual Report, p.14.
[319] Weyerhaeuser claims it does not export old growth.
[320] Weyerhaeuser, Nov./Dec. 1991, p.2.

exports by February 20, 1990.[321] This meant Weyerhaeuser would no longer export from Oregon and could therefore once again bid on Forest Service timber sales. Behind this decision is public policy which states that companies which export logs from a geographic area (technically called a "working circle") may not bid on Forest Service timber sales in that same region.[322]

ECONOMIC IMPACT OF EXPORTS

Loss of Mill Jobs Due to the Exportation of Raw Logs

Raw log exports have a major influence on employment in the timber industry. Numerous studies have attempted to determine the number of jobs which would be gained (or lost) through a partial or total ban on raw log exports. Their conclusions range from the possibility of a ban adding 15,000 jobs to that of a ban costing 2,000 jobs. These different numbers are based in part on different definitions, assumptions, and economic models. The results of a few of these studies are as follows.

- A joint U.S. Forest Service/Bureau of Land Management study concluded a private log export ban could save 15,000 jobs.[323]

- Gus Kuehne, who represents the Northwest Independent Forest Manufacturers Association, suggested a partial ban would create 5,000 direct and indirect jobs.[324]

- A 1990 study by the Washington State Employment Security Division reported that every million board feet exported cost seven direct and 14 indirect jobs.[325]

---

[321] AP, Nov. 28, 1990.
[322] By Forest Service regulation, 36 C.F.R. 221.25.
[323] U.S. Forest Service and Bureau of Land Management, 1990.
[324] Nogaki, June 11, 1990.
[325] Washington State Employment Security Division, 1990.

- The Washington Citizens for World Trade (financed by the major exporters, including Weyerhaeuser and Plum Creek, and staffed by former Plum Creek vice-president Nick Kirkmire) proposed that a ban would cost 1,500 direct and indirect jobs.[326]

- A study by the Washington Citizens for World Trade, the International Longshoremen's, and the Warehousemen's Union suggested a ban would cost 2,000 jobs, and cost the Washington Department of Natural Resources $86 million in timber receipts and Washington state $4 million in taxes.[327]

- Donald Flora, an economist with the U.S. Forest Service, stated that a ban could add 450 or lose 110 jobs, depending on the level of automation of the mills involved.[328]

Despite the wide range of numbers, it is clear that with one out of four logs in Washington and Oregon being exported, exports are a major factor in the region's timber supply.

Balance of Trade

President Reagan's final budget proposal, submitted January 1989 and endorsed by President Bush, proposed ending this country's 21-year-old restriction on raw log exports from federal lands, stating it would increase federal receipts up to $200 million by the third year. Other estimates of the increased revenues, including one by the Congressional Research Service, were much lower, about $30 million annually.[329] As we shall see, federal log exports were ended in 1990-1992.

Although there are those who argue that raw log exports are a way to significantly reduce the trade deficit, this is clearly not the case.

---

[326] Nogaki, June 11, 1990.
[327] *Seattle Times*, Jan. 5, 1990.
[328] Flora, 1990.
[329] Gorte, April 22, 1991.

International trade in timber products, and specifically in raw logs, is a small part of total U.S. trade – less than 0.6 cent in 1986. The total trade deficit in 1988 was $139.5 billion.[330] In 1988 all exports from the United States were worth $310 billion. Raw logs were worth $2.2 billion, or less than one percent of all commodities exported.[331] The nation's trade deficit cannot be resolved by exporting the nation's forests.

The situation is similar, though not so extreme, for the Pacific Northwest and for Washington state. In 1990 total softwood exports from Washington were worth $1.3 billion, which falls a distant second to airplanes ($15 billion), and accounts for only 3.5 percent of the state's exports. Even if Boeing, which accounts for nearly half of total state exports, were excepted from that figure, softwood exports would still only account for less than 7 percent.[332]

Finally, while exporting $4.249 *billion* worth of raw logs in 1988, the United States imported $12.144 billion worth of lumber, plywood, veneer, particleboard, hardboard, paper and paperboard, and only $18.1 *million* worth of raw logs.[333] Thus in forest products, the United States is a net exporter of natural resources and a net importer of processed products.

The real question regarding the balance of trade argument for reducing or increasing raw log exports is whether the importers of raw logs will shift to greater purchases of value-added products. The shift is technically possible, and the log importers have few alternative sources – Canada and most tropical nations prohibit log exports (some even ban lumber exports).[334] On the other hand, the Japanese and

---

[330]   *World Almanac*, 1991, p.161, citing U.S. Department of Commerce Office of Industry and Trade Information.

[331]   Ulrich, 1990, p.20, citing U.S. Department of Commerce Bureau of the Census, and the U.S. Council of Economic Advisors.

[332]   Washington State 1991 Data Book, p.28. These figures are for the entire state. Timber exports clearly are more important to the economies of some of the individual ports; for example, about three-quarters of the ships calling at the Port of Everett carry away logs (Wilhelm, July 29, 1991).

[333]   Ulrich, 1990, p.20.

[334]   British Columbia has restricted the export of unprocessed timber since 1901 (Hines, 1987, p.11). The Malaysian island states of Sabah and Sarawak are exceptions to the prohibition of exporting raw logs, and their supplies are likely to be depleted within about a decade. Chile and New Zealand export logs, but their quality is generally unacceptable to the Japanese market. Some companies are

others may choose not to purchase value-added products for political reasons (e.g., to express displeasure at a log export ban).[335]

The Move Towards Value-added Products

In 1991 a study done for Washington state recommended that small and medium-sized companies respond to timber supply restrictions by offering more value-added manufacturing.[336] The major timber companies have been quick to move in this direction as well. In 1990, for example, Plum Creek and Sumitomo, a Japanese conglomerate involved in several Pacific Northwest timber operations, opened a joint venture in Spokane, Washington. It manufactures glue-laminated posts for the exacting Japanese housing market, prices its products competitively, and has the potential to employ 100 people.[337] Plum Creek is also marketing medium-density fiberboard products to the highly restrictive European market.[338]

While encouraging, the creation of value-added industries leaves the fundamental problems of overcutting unresolved.

Further, despite the increasing number of studies recommending that small and medium-sized mills move towards value-added products,[339] these are the mills which find it most difficult to retool.[340]

Those companies which can make the switch are primarily those able to invest in the new technologies and plants – including, once again, the major land-grant timber companies. Many owners of small mills do not have the capital to compete in the value-added market, nor do they have the national or international marketing operations to fully take advantage of value-added products.

---

attempting to move into Siberia, but there exist technical and environmental difficulties with this (Gorte, Oct. 1, 1992).

[335]   Gorte, Oct. 1, 1992.

[336]   Nogaki, June 27, 1991; and Virgin, June 27, 1991.

[337]   *Seattle Daily Journal of Commerce*, Feb. 19, 1990.

[338]   Plum Creek, 1990 Annual Report, p.4.

[339]   See, for example, Jensen International, 1991. This study, done for the Washington State Department of Trade and Economic Development, was executed by Paul Jensen, who formerly directed export marketing and sales for Plum Creek.

[340]   Anderson and Olson, 1991, pp.79-80; and Polzin, 1990.

The result is that the Pacific Northwest timber industry is increasingly falling into the hands of a few companies – largely Congress's land-grant-based timber companies.

A BRIEF CHRONOLOGY OF LOG EXPORT RESTRICTIONS SINCE 1968

Following is a brief history of log export restrictions spurred by the recognition of exports' injurious consequences.

In 1968 the Morse Amendment limited the export of logs from federal lands (Forest Service and BLM) in the West to 350 million board feet.[341] In 1973 this quantity was dropped to zero, with exemptions to be determined by the Secretary of Agriculture and the Secretary of the Interior. This restriction had to be renewed annually as part of the annual Congressional appropriations process.[342]

Also in 1973, Senators Frank Church (D-ID), Bob Packwood (R-OR), and Alan Cranston (D-CA) tried to restrict private exports. They were opposed by Weyerhaeuser and others, and the attempt failed.

Until 1984 Alaska, California, Idaho, and Oregon prohibited the exportation of logs from state lands.[343] In 1984 the U.S. Supreme Court ruled that Alaska's restriction of the export of state-owned timber was an unconstitutional burden on interstate trade.[344] In June 1984, California stated it would continue to restrict exports until a court or the state Legislature told them to stop.[345]

Idaho stopped enforcement of the restrictions in 1984.[346] On April 10, 1989, it passed a new law restricting exports of logs from state lands, reserving 95 percent of the 200 million board feet annual cut for mills in Idaho. Proponents said that business and personal taxes paid by Idaho sawmills offset returns from higher prices paid for exported logs by a factor of nearly five to one. Senator James McClure (R-ID)

---

[341] The Morse Amendment to the Foreign Assistance Act of 1968 (82 Stat. 966).

[342] This is the amendment Reagan and Bush tried to repeal in 1989, saying its repeal would decrease the trade deficit.

[343] Hines, 1987, p.8.

[344] South-Central Timber Development v. Wunnicke, May 22, 1984; see Hines (1987, pp.8-10) for the states' reactions to the decision.

[345] Hines, 1987, p.9.

[346] Idaho Attorney General Opinion 84-9.

pressed for U.S. legislation validating Idaho's restrictions and for making the federal log export ban permanent.[347]

Oregon also stopped enforcement of its restrictions after the 1984 Supreme Court decision. In 1989 Oregon voters approved in a referendum, by a nine-to-one margin, a new permanent ban on the exportation of state-owned logs, at the same time calling on Congress to make the ban on federal exports permanent. Non-exporting timber companies spent $800,000 on the campaign to get the measure passed.[348] The ban was contingent on approval from Congress.

In April 1989, following the lead of his state, Senator Bob Packwood (R-OR) introduced legislation to permanently extend the 21-year-old ban on federal log exports and to let states impose similar bans on state logs. Senators James McClure (R-ID), Conrad Burns (R-MT), and Ted Stevens (R-AK) joined Packwood, who also had the support of various environmental, labor, and business groups, as well as non-exporting companies such as Boise Cascade. Similar legislation in the House, sponsored by Representative Peter DeFazio (D-OR), died in the Foreign Affairs Committee. DeFazio reintroduced his measure later, with co-sponsors Jolene Unsoeld (D-WA), Les AuCoin (D-WA), Larry Craig (R-ID), and Richard Stallings (D-ID). Congress approved this legislation in 1990 as the Forest Resources Conservation and Shortages Relief Act of 1990 (FRCSRA).[349] FRCSRA banned the export of unprocessed timber from state or other public lands in contiguous states west of the 100th meridian, except for Washington state lands, where 75 percent were banned[350] until September of 1992, when Department of Commerce regulation prohibited the export of all raw logs from state lands in Washington.[351] On May 4, 1993, the Ninth Circuit Court of Appeals ruled that the 1990 federal FRCSRA ban on exporting raw logs from Western state lands was a violation of

---

[347]   Connelly, April 11, 1989.
[348]   AP, June 28, 1989.
[349]   104 Stat. 629.
[350]   16 U.S.C. Sec. 620.
[351]   Schaefer, Sept. 18, 1992.

Washington state's autonomy,[352] but in June 1993 Congress reinstated the ban.[353]

GETTING AROUND THE BAN: SUBSTITUTIONS

Corporations sidestep federal log export prohibitions through a variety of substitution schemes. In "second party substitution" the first party purchases federal timber and sells it to a second party which then exports the trees. This was outlawed by a 1974 U.S. Forest Service regulation.[354] According to a U.S. Forest Service report, this regulation

> precludes the purchaser from substituting or replacing private exported timber with National Forest timber. The regulations do not prevent others (third parties) from buying National Forest timber from the purchaser and substituting it for the private timber **they** export. This practice is termed "third party substitution."[355]

The Forest Service and timber industry organizations estimate third party substitution involves 100 million board feet per year in the Western United States – a figure considered low by others. The U.S. Forest Service believes it cannot enforce a ban on third party substitution without additional authority.[356]

In testimony before a Senate committee on November 7, 1989, U.S. Representative Pat Williams (D-MT) described some of the effects of substitution by Plum Creek by saying that "this problem has significant financial, technical ramifications, and the people that are suffering those ramifications are the workers that worked for small timber companies in places like Montana."[357]

---

[352]   The violation is under the tenth Amendment to the U.S. Constitution; the Court of Appeals also cited a 1992 Supreme Court ruling that Congress cannot require states to enact a federal regulatory program (*Seattle Times*, May 5, 1993, p.A1,A3).

[353]   AP, June 18, 1993. The federal government now administers the ban.

[354]   36 C.F.R. 221.25.

[355]   Hines, 1987, p.2.

[356]   Hines, 1987, p.3; and Gahr, 1990, pp.5-6.

[357]   Williams, Nov. 7, 1989.

FRCSRA phased out direct substitution in Washington and Oregon, and all forms of substitution in Oregon. It allowed for 50 million board feet of indirect (third party) substitution of federal logs in Washington.

Regulations and laws banning raw log exports from federal lands do not prevent companies such as Plum Creek from exporting logs from Northern Pacific grant lands and using resulting profits to bid on and gain access to public timber – much of which is sold at a loss to the taxpayer. The public's forests, conditionally granted to a railroad, are converted via log exports to profits that, rather than support the railroad, are used to buy more public timber.[358]

While curtailing some forms of substitution, FRCSRA made other forms explicitly legal for the first time. One of the main beneficiaries of this legalized substitution was Plum Creek.

Plum Creek: a Study in Legalized Substitutions

Forest Service regulations permit bids on public timber only from companies that have not exported private timber from that area for two years. Though a major exporter of old-growth logs, Plum Creek asked on December 18, 1990, to be allowed to bid on federal timber sales in eastern Washington and Idaho. It asked that the Forest Service consider the company's operations as existing in separate geographical entities called "sourcing units."[359] Though environmentalists argued that all Plum Creek operations are interdependent, the Forest Service recommended allowing the company to bid on federal timber.

Environmentalists appealed the U.S. Forest Service decision in favor of Plum Creek, arguing:

- Plum Creek's bids would increase logging pressures, increases not accounted for in current ten-year management plans for the region's National Forests;

- the FRCSRA regulations would circumvent the National Environmental Policy Act (NEPA) by not evaluating

---

[358]   Palmer, 1991. The public subsidy comes in the form of below-cost timber sales, where the Forest Service spends more on timber sale administration and road construction than it receives for the timber.

[359]   Palmer, 1991.

the environmental consequences of granting sourcing
areas;

• Plum Creek is an example of a log exporting company
using FRCSRA, a law designed to relieve timber
shortage, to gain rights to bid on public timber; and

• Plum Creek did not publicly disclose corporate data on
log exports as required by FRCSRA.[360]

On April 16, 1991, the Department of Agriculture's administrative
law judge Victor Palmer agreed with the U.S. Forest Service that Plum
Creek's eastern Washington and Idaho "sourcing areas" were
geographically and economically separate from Plum Creek's export
operations. Judge Palmer's decision, which had been prepared in
advance of the hearing by Plum Creek's attorneys on their letterhead,
allowed Plum Creek to acquire public trees in the Pacific Northwest
while exporting Pacific Northwest raw logs.[361]

In this case, FRCSRA, a log export reform law, was used to
legitimize substitution. Plum Creek, whose main assets are public
lands given in exchange for railroad operations, was set up to divert
those assets away from the railroad and toward corporate profit. It
exports public trust trees to foreign buyers and uses the profits to bid
against domestic mills for increasingly scarce public trees.

ENDING LOG EXPORTS

Though banning private log exports would provide approximately
three billion board feet per year for domestic processing,[362] federal
policy has actually encouraged raw log exports through tax breaks
totaling $100 million to companies registered as Domestic International
Sales Corporations (since the 1970s), or Foreign Sales Corporations

---

[360]   Osborn, April 16, 1991.
[361]   Palmer, Oct. 1991.
[362]   Anderson and Olson, p.76; and K.R. Thomas, 1989.

(since the 1986 tax law).[363] The budget bill passed in August 1993 repealed the FSC tax break; $270 million of the $393 million in revenues that will be generated over five years are to be directed to help timber communities.[364]

One option to increase domestic processing would be to further shift tax incentives away from the export market and towards domestic value-added processing.[365] This could be done in the form of an inverse tax: the more processing is done domestically, the less tax is paid.

Recent Efforts to Ban or Curtail the Exportation of Raw Logs

There have been many bills proposed in the past few years attempting to halt the export of logs from private lands. A few of these are as follows.

- U.S. Representative Peter DeFazio (D-OR) introduced a bill in September 1990 to ban private log exports, with exemptions for small woodlot owners of less than 320 acres. He cited a U.S. Forest Service estimate that a private log export ban could save 15,000 jobs in Oregon and Washington.[366]

- U.S. Senator Mark Hatfield (R-OR) proposed a capital gains tax break for private owners who sell their logs domestically. U.S. Representative Jolene Unsoeld (D-WA) prepared similar legislation in the U.S. House.

- In September 1991, DeFazio and three others of the Washington and Oregon Congressional delegations

---

[363]   26 C.F.R. 1.991-1; FSC definition and regulations are at 26 C.F.R. 1.921-2. Weyerhaeuser vice-president Charles Bingham, in testimony at President Clinton's Forest Conference on April 2, 1993, in Portland, Oregon, stated that the tax break for Weyerhaeuser in 1992 was worth $19 million. See Weyerhaeuser's 1993 Annual Report, p. 57.

[364]   McDermott, Aug. 6, 1993.

[365]   Scates, June 21, 1992.

[366]   Schaefer, Aug. 31, 1990.

introduced a bill that would have allowed states to impose a tax of up to 10 percent on log exports. DeFazio suggested the Commerce Secretary be required to restrict log exports when there is a critical shortage. Weyerhaeuser opposed this bill.[367]

- A June 1992 bill co-sponsored by Senators Pat Leahy (D-VT) and Brock Adams (D-WA) would have allowed states to restrict private log exports.

- A 1991 bill put forward by Representative Pete Stark (D-CA) would have reduced the FSC and DISC tax incentives for private log exports.[368] The FSC tax break was repealed in August 1993, as stated above.

- A bill to ban private log exports, sponsored by DeFazio, failed the House in July 1994.

Opposition to restricting the export of "private" raw logs has been consistent and intense. George Weyerhaeuser told the Seattle Rotary Club that restriction on federal land should not apply to privately owned land. Weyerhaeuser lobbyist Fred Benson wrote that because of Stark's bill Weyerhaeuser would withhold support for a separate compromise bill protecting ancient forests. Weyerhaeuser's position received support from at least five of Washington's Representatives.[369]

Plum Creek opposes private log export restrictions, saying they would glut the domestic market while sending Asian buyers to Chile,

---

[367]   Council on Economic Priorities report on Weyerhaeuser, 1992, p.17.
[368]   AP, June 18, 1993.
[369]   Healy, 1990; and Schaefer, June 2, 1992; and Scates, June 21, 1992.
         The Representatives included Norm Dicks (D), Al Swift (D), Sid Morrison (R), John Miller (R), and Rod Chandler (R). The support provided to Weyerhaeuser by much of the Washington delegation is reminiscent of the support by the Washington delegation for the legislation that, in exchange for the establishment of Mt. Rainier National Park, ceded large tracts of the public's forests to the railroads (30 Stat. 597, July 1, 1898, as amended in 1906).

New Zealand, Canada, and Russia.[370] In its 1990 Annual Report, it urged investors to "write their U.S. Senators and Representatives asking them to oppose any restrictions on the export of privately grown agricultural [sic] products, especially timber."[371]

Since 1864 Congress has listened carefully to investors in the Northern Pacific and its corporate heirs. The recent increase in the restriction of log exports shows that Congress is beginning to listen to others, including owners of domestic mills, the workers in those mills, and a concerned public which decries the role of exports in the destruction of Pacific Northwest forests and communities.

FURTHER OPTIONS

In 1989 the U.S. Congressional Research Service concluded that a ban on private log exports would be constitutional, but such a restriction of interstate and international trade would require action by both federal and state governments.[372]

The December 1993 passage of the North American Free Trade Agreement and the General Agreement on Tariffs and Trade, both of which "harmonize" international trade standards and reduce trade barriers, may affect whether and how any restrictions can be placed on the export of raw logs from private (or even public) lands. The results of implementation remain to be seen.

Even if NAFTA and GATT do not prevent the restriction of log exports, existing pressures such as those put forth by Weyerhaeuser against restraint of trade suggest that there may be a politically more expedient option than an outright ban: federal and/or state tariffs on raw logs. A tariff on private log exports would make more timber available for domestic processing and provide revenue for state and local governments.[373] After British Columbia imposed a tax equal to the "export premium" – the difference in prices paid for exported and

---

[370]   Titone, May 1, 1990. For a counter to this argument, see Gorte, April 22, 1991.

[371]   Plum Creek, 1990 Annual Report, insert between pp.6-7.

[372]   Thomas, 1989.

[373]   Sept. 25, 1991 bill introduced (Council on Economic Priorities report on Weyerhaeuser, 1992, p.17).

domestically processed logs – log exports virtually halted and lumber production increased.[374]

Another option suggested by Senator Hatfield (R-OR) is a preferential capital gains tax treatment for timber processed domestically. Critics have objected to the loss of tax revenue and to excessive subsidies for the timber industry.[375]

Yet another option to restrict the exportation of raw logs from railroad grant lands might be to amend Congress's 1864 and 1870 grants. This would be consistent with Congress's authority to amend legislation.

---

[374] Anderson and Olson, 1991, p.77.
[375] Anderson and Olson, 1991, p.77.

OPTIONS TO INTERVENE

REINING IN CONGRESS'S LAND-GRANT LEGACY

We have explored many of the unintended effects of Congress's 1864 and 1870 grants. These include the overcutting and exporting of the forests of the Pacific Northwest, with consequent environmental degradation and economic dislocation; increased pressure to overcut the public's National Forests; the effects of forest fragmentation caused by the checkerboards embedded within the National Forests; and the weakening of the U. S. Forest Service as a professional agency.

There are, however, alternatives that Congress, other governmental agencies, or individuals may wish to investigate in order to resolve or at least to mitigate these problems. These alternatives include an analysis of the cooperative relationship that exists among major timber corporations and state and federal governments, a strengthening of state forest practices acts, and actions at the federal level.

One of the possible actions at the federal level would be the passage of a national private forest practices act. Another would be for the federal government to acquire, through purchase or exchange, tracts of Pacific Northwest forests currently claimed by major timber companies. Since many of these large timber companies are based on the Northern Pacific railroad land grants, a third option would be for Congress to amend the grants, as reserved in grant legislation and authorized by the U.S. Constitution.

CONTINUING "COOPERATIVE" FORESTRY

In 1924, with the passage of the Clarke-McNary Act,[376] the federal government committed itself to a "cooperative" relationship with timber corporations. This cooperative relationship guaranteed that even though many of the National Forests contain intermingled ownership – because of the 1864 and 1870 railroad land grants, over which Congress maintains oversight – the Forest Service would not be allowed to provide oversight of how "private" lands were managed. Congress took this action despite timber companies having cut down the forests in the Great Lakes region and New England, and despite clear warnings by Gifford Pinchot, a founder of American forestry, who in 1919 recommended that the federal government assume a regulatory role towards timber corporations. He stated bluntly in the *Journal of Forestry* that "destructive lumbering on private timberlands is working a grave injury to the public interest and must be stopped."[377]

The cooperative relationship was questioned in the 1933 Copeland Report, named for the U.S. Senator who requested the report, which is considered the most thorough assessment of American forests to its time.[378] Seventy years later, the land-grant forests of the Pacific Northwest are overcut. When an entire region is overcut, the public should seriously question the efficacy of the "cooperative" relationship. Through the 1980s, public frustration with corporate forest practices grew.

The major liquidation of forests on the land-grant checkerboards from Yellowstone National Park to Seattle demonstrates the failure of the cooperative relationship established by Congress. Timber companies often argue that destructive forest practices are things of the past and that their techniques are improving.[379] A prominent recent example of this argument has been Plum Creek's proclaimed conversion to so-called "New Forestry."[380]

---

[376] Cooperative Forest Management Act of 1924 (43 Stat. 653), replaced in 1978 by the Cooperative Forestry Assistance Act (92 Stat. 365).

[377] Pinchot, 1919.

[378] U.S. Senate, 1933.

[379] For a thorough examination by a biologist of the believability of such pleas for understanding and time, see Ehrenfeld, 1978, especially Chapter 3, "Reality."

[380] For example, see Farney, June 18, 1990.

New Forestry, as envisioned by scientists such as former Forest Service ecologist Jerry Franklin, is a theory that trees can be cut while still leaving the forest structure intact. Proponents are attempting to develop cutting methods that leave some of the trees standing, shape the cuts to fit local terrain, and give additional consideration to riparian and other sensitive areas. They also suggest leaving snags (standing dead trees) and downed logs. The standing trees, snags, and logs would remain on the site through the next timber rotation – 50 to 100 years.[381]

There is little research available which shows the effectiveness of New Forestry, and it will be many years before quantifiable results of experimentation with New Forestry become available. Because of this, there is disagreement among foresters about the benefits of New Forestry.

The effect of New Forestry on levels of cutting would likely be significant, according to Richard Fairbanks, a timber sale planner on the Willamette National Forest in Oregon, who has worked in Forest Service resource planning and fire management for 20 years. Speaking of New Forestry, he says:

> [A] large area is clearcut, with snags and woody debris retained in volumes which closely mimic a stand-replacing fire. By implication, of course, a large clearcut must be complemented with thousands of acres of old forest, if it is to truly emulate natural landscape patterns. This is a basic problem with most New Forestry techniques. They do not meet the needs of the agency and its corporate clients in this respect because they will result in harvest levels far lower than the ten percent drop predicted by the [Forest Service] Chief's new policy on Ecosystem Management.[382]

It is unknown whether Plum Creek's use of New Forestry will succeed in reducing environmental degradation or overcutting; it is possible that it will do no more than allow current trends to continue. There is no independent corroboration of Plum Creek's claims.

---

[381] Franklin, 1989, p.43.
[382] Fairbanks, 1992.

Further, Plum Creek practices New Forestry on only 15 percent of the land it controls.[383] Also, since New Forestry is a theory instead of a strict prescription for practice, Plum Creek has often been able to claim it is practicing New Forestry while continuing the company's preexisting policies. For example, Plum Creek's corporate biologist Lorin Hicks mentions a New Forestry stand in which Plum Creek will "return in 15 to 20 years and remove the trees we saved the first time."[384] Thus, the experiment with New Forestry becomes just another "shelterwood" cut – essentially a two-stage clearcut – with Plum Creek entering the same site twice. The company's claims of "New Forestry" have not resulted in an end of overcutting.[385]

American forest policy has allowed Plum Creek and its predecessor, Burlington Northern, to cut down massive areas of forest. Plum Creek is not alone in this. Weyerhaeuser claims there is virtually no old growth left on its holdings.[386] Potlatch has a gap in its timber supply. Champion admitted to a "hellacious hole" in timber supply.[387] What happened in the Northeast and in the Midwest has happened again in the Pacific Northwest. The Clarke-McNary Act and the "cooperative" relationship between corporations and the federal government has allowed overcutting to continue.

STATE REGULATIONS

Although there are laws which allow the federal government to regulate cutting on the national forests, the government has no such regulatory power over state and private lands. In the absence of a nationwide forest practices act, responsibility for regulating corporate cutting has fallen by default upon state governments. States can influence cutting directly through forest practices acts or indirectly through laws to protect water and wildlife.

Are the Pacific Northwestern states capable of regulating the cutting of Congress's land-grant forests within their borders? One need only look at what has happened to the checkerboard lands

---

[383]   Plum Creek, 1993 Annual Report, p.10.
[384]   AP, Aug. 29, 1991.
[385]   Farney, June 18, 1990.
[386]   Taylor and Werner, Nov. 10, 1990.
[387]   Manning, Oct. 16, 1988.

between Yellowstone National Park and the Pacific Ocean to see that the states have not protected forests and forest-dependent communities from overcutting. Current state laws do not work.

Montana has no state forest practices regulations.[388] Idaho does have regulations, as does Washington.[389] Washington's are the most stringent of the two, but it was not until June 1992 that Washington even restricted the size of individual clearcuts – to 240 acres. Without meaningful restrictions on the proximity and cumulative effects of nearby cuts, the restriction is still virtually meaningless.

Further, the Washington regulations, which were approved and released on June 26, 1992, did not take effect until August 1, 1992. Those who obtained forest practices permits before August 1 were able to receive a three-year grace period to bypass the new restrictions.[390] Thousands did.

Washington has tried twice to negotiate "New Forestry" regulations, including cutting levels, and both times the process has been difficult and has achieved only minimal success.[391] The power of the timber industry is underscored by the statement of then-Washington state House Natural Resources Committee Chair Jennifer Belcher,[392] telling how lobbyists for timber corporations killed proposed state regulations: "The industry came in here and told me they had taken away my committee votes. They said, 'It's our way or the highway,' and so it's dead as far as I'm concerned."[393]

Another tool available to states for blunting the environmental consequences of overcutting is federally sanctioned protection of clean water and its beneficial uses. Federal legislation such as the Clean Water Act specifically requires states to implement regulatory authority to protect the waters within their borders.

---

[388]   For discussion, see Manning, 1991; see also Anez, Dec. 10, 1988.

[389]   Generally, WAC 222.

[390]   Taylor, June 27, 1992.

[391]   The negotiations were the so-called Timber, Fish, and Wildlife (or "TFW"), which resulted in an agreement and new regulations in 1987, and the Sustainable Forestry Roundtable, which never came to agreement.

[392]   In 1992, Belcher became Washington Commissioner of Public Lands and head of the Department of Natural Resources, which regulates timber cutting on private lands.

[393]   AP, March 6, 1991.

An example of the inability of states to use clean water legislation to provide meaningful oversight of corporate cutting is provided by Idaho's experiences with the Clean Water Act. In Idaho, timber companies effectively convinced the Legislature to pass legislation in 1986 that was vetoed by Governor John Evans. They tried again with similar legislation in 1988, this time vetoed by Governor Cecil Andrus. This legislation, labeled "the dirty water act" by conservationists, would have adopted an antidegradation policy which contained no implementation language, no public involvement, and no site-specific evaluations of water quality impacts.[394]

Following his veto, Andrus directed that mediation occur to resolve the clean water debate. An agreement was reached in September 1988, called Idaho's Antidegradation Policy.[395]

In 1990 timber company lobbyists effectively thwarted implementation even of this compromise antidegradation agreement, to which they are a party, by convincing the Idaho Legislature to block necessary funding.[396]

The controlling of rates of cutting and environmental degradation on the railroad land-grant holdings in the Pacific Northwest by the respective states has not been successful. It *is* technically possible for states to regulate cutting within their borders, but given the immense political and economic resources of the major timber companies based on Congress's Northern Pacific land grant, it is at the same time manifestly unrealistic to expect sparsely populated states such as Idaho and Montana, or even Washington, to legislate and enforce protection of the land-grant-based forests within their boundaries. Forest protection, if it comes, will likely fall to Congress, which

---

[394]   Idaho Conservation League, April 1992.

[395]   Klahr, 1992. Klahr's response to the agreement is typical of that of conservationists. She has written, "But what really burns, what really irritates the public and the activists, is that the entire purpose, the heart of the matter, *antidegradation* — stopping damage to watershed resources *before* it occurs, restoring degraded watersheds, and ensuring that the environmental risks associated with nonpoint source pollution are economically justified — has not happened. The staff, the image, the paperwork, the meetings, the rules and regulations . . . these are all part of the bureaucracy, but do nothing for the resource **on-the-ground**" (Klahr, 1992, italic and bold in the original).

[396]   Hinson, Feb. 2, 1990; see also AP, April 25, 1990.

created the railroad grants in the first place and unleashed unintended corporate empires on the Pacific Northwest.

OPPORTUNITIES FOR CONGRESS

Federal Forest Practices Act

The slim prospects of state regulations leave protection against overcutting to the federal government. Through the years, proposals have repeatedly been made for federal forest practices regulations governing the treatment of all forests within the country's borders.

The Pacific Northwest has been overcut, as were the Great Lakes and the New England regions before it. The cooperative relationship established by the 1924 Clarke-McNary Act has failed the forests and the forest-dependent communities of the Pacific Northwest. Congress could, therefore, review the fundamental relationship between the American people and large timber companies. Such a goal would not be punitive, but rather a national effort to prevent further overcutting of the Pacific Northwest and to prevent other regions – the Southern and Northeastern United States – from being overcut again. It would constitute an effort to intervene in the migratory nature of timber companies, thereby protecting the nation's forests and forest-dependent communities.

One possible intervention would be a Congressional amendment to the Northern Pacific grant legislation. Congress could regulate cutting on all granted lands, thus recognizing the continuing obligation of the grantees to the American public and Congress's own obligation to safeguard the public interest.

Reforming Incentives

In addition to regulations concerning forest practices, Congress could review the tax incentives which drive many of the current forest practices. For example, Congress has repealed the tax incentives for exporting raw logs; it could also review the tax-exempt status for Plum Creek and other natural resource-extracting limited partnerships.[397] In place of current tax law, Congress could establish incentives which reward sound and sustainable forest practices.

Reviewing the Land Grant

The failed policies of the past have carried the Pacific Northwest to this forest crisis. An acute part of this crisis revolves around the railroad checkerboard embedded within the National Forests, part of the legacy of Congress's Northern Pacific land grants.

Congressional oversight of the 1864 and 1870 Northern Pacific land grants has been exercised in the past. Between 1870 and 1890, numerous attempts were made by members of Congress to revest the land grants associated with many of the land-grant railroads, including those associated with Northern Pacific.[398] These culminated in a general forfeiture act in 1890, which returned to the public domain two million acres of land previously granted to Northern Pacific.[399] This revestiture "was a weak palliative to men . . . who had struggled for so long to secure a law which would restore appreciable portions of the railroad grants to the public domain."[400]

Federal oversight to protect the public interest was again exercised in 1924, when President Calvin Coolidge called for a thorough inquiry into the land grants. This resulted in the Congressional investigation of 1924 to 1928 and the subsequent 1930-40 federal lawsuit against Northern Pacific.[401] Further, in 1981, Congress requested that attorney Pamela Baldwin of the Congressional Research Service assess the current status of Congressional oversight of the Northern Pacific land grants. Her conclusions included the fact that, "Congress may always amend earlier legislation – a fact that was expressly reiterated in Section 20 of the 1864 Northern Pacific legislation."[402] Further, Baldwin provided several action alternatives for Congressional consideration. Among them was the possibility that Congress could

---

[397]   Gillie, May 27, 1990.

[398]   See, for example, Schwinden, 1950, pp.69-87.

[399]   26 Stat. 496. In the 1890 Act, 11 railroads forfeited 5.6 million acres (Ellis, 1946, pp.54-55).

[400]   Schwinden, 1950, p.85.

[401]   U.S. Congress, 1924-1928; U.S. v. NP, 311 U.S. 317 (1940).

[402]   Baldwin, 1981, p.39.

"find that conditions of the land grants had been violated and revest title to some or all of the lands in the United States."[403]

It is clear that the American people, through Congress, retain legal and practical oversight of and interest in Congress's 1864 and 1870 Northern Pacific land grants.

ELIMINATING THE LAND-GRANT CHECKERBOARD

As shown earlier, it is impossible to manage National Forests on an ecosystem basis when millions of acres of privately claimed, mismanaged, railroad grant lands are embedded within. One step toward mitigating the current crisis of management in the National Forests of the Pacific Northwest would be to eliminate the land-grant checkerboards.

Solutions to Checkerboards Problems

There are three main ways the federal government could eliminate the land-grant checkerboard inholdings within the National Forests. All involve the acquisition of these properties. The options are exchange, purchase, and revestment.

(1) Exchanges

There are numerous problems with the concept of exchanging National Forest land for checkerboard inholdings. The first has to do with the lack of effective forestry practices policies. For example, since Montana does not regulate cutting on private or corporate lands, the consolidation of lands claimed by Plum Creek in Montana would merely shift, but not end, forest destruction. It would also provide an unfair competitive advantage to Plum Creek's mills in the region by giving them land which had until then been open to their competitors. Finally, the loss of National Forest lands and the increase in lands under Plum Creek control within county boundaries would cost the county governments involved significant revenue: nearby National Forest lands sometimes net counties more than seven times as much

---

[403]   Baldwin, 1981, p.40.

through federal "in-lieu" payments as counties receive through corporate taxes.[404]

A Forest Service memo is particularly revealing about the untoward consequences of exchanges:

> I think that in the long haul the problems may be fewer, the costs may be less and it is probably more ethical to buy the BN [now Plum Creek] lands outright, probably through condemnation proceedings, rather than try to exchange for lands in areas where a BN subsidiary is involved in competitive bidding with long established wood products companies. Ethically and morally I question any voluntary action on the part of the Forest Service which places existing mills in jeopardy. These mills have been established and maintained by the timber base we are now considering for exchange for their dominant competitor. . . . I suggest that before we spend any more time and money looking at tentative preliminary packages for exchange, an effort be made to get informal or even formal consultation with interested groups and individuals other than BN officials. I believe what will be found through this process would support my opinion that it is simply not possible, with today's level of public involvement, to consummate an exchange in which considerable acreage of timber producing land is removed from a Forest's timber base.[405]

Despite these problems with exchanges – and the additional problem that in previous land exchanges with Burlington Resources, mineral rights were retained by Burlington Northern, Meridian Minerals, or other Burlington Northern spin-offs, thus guaranteeing

---

[404]   Applegate, 1979, p.68.
[405]   Memorandum to Regional Forester, from Dave Minister, Program Coordinator, U.S. Forest Service, June 3, 1977. Published in "Forest, Rail Land Swap Is Opposed," *Billings Gazette*, Aug. 27, 1978. Reprinted in Applegate, 1979, footnote 248.

that ownership consolidation was not accomplished[406] – the Forest Service has continued to exchange lands with Plum Creek and others.

(2) Purchase

Another option would be for the federal government to purchase the checkerboards. Secretary of Agriculture Henry Wallace suggested in 1933 that due to corporate cut-and-run policies, state and federal governments purchase cutover corporate lands. With a reformed Forest Service committed to the long-term health of forest ecosystems, these acquisitions could guarantee state-of-the-art regeneration techniques.

The costs could be large if Plum Creek's valuation is used. Plum Creek values the land and timber alone at $527 million. It values its manufacturing facilities at $163 million.[407] The $527 million, of course, would not include the checkerboards claimed by Potlatch, Weyerhaeuser, and other land-grant-based corporations.

It might be possible for funding to come partially or temporarily from private sources, perhaps from funds raised through taxation of the timber industry itself, such as a specific tax on raw log exports. In August of 1993, Congress set a precedent for this by repealing the FSC tax break and directing the resulting revenues to forest-dependent communities.

Another possible source for private funding would be The Nature Conservancy (TNC). TNC attempted to buy large tracts of checkerboards in the Gallatin National Forest, but Plum Creek sold

---

[406]   Applegate, 1979, p.69. The Burlington Resources spin-off Meridian Minerals retains the subsurface rights to Plum Creek lands (Plum Creek, May 1989, p.43). Much of the coal has been transferred to Great Northern Properties L.P. (Dow Jones, Oct. 28, 1992).

    Unfortunately, these figures account only for the surface rights. The subsurface rights are for the most part claimed by spin-offs of Burlington Northern/ Burlington Resources. The value of the subsurface rights (for coal and other minerals) are unknown, but is certainly far greater than the value of the timber.

[407]   Plum Creek, 1993 Annual Report, p.18.

instead to a timber company.[408] One difficulty with TNC purchasing the checkerboards is that TNC's budget is only $156 million for the entire country, and it has acquired only five million acres nationwide since its founding in 1951.[409] TNC's largest purchase has been the Gray Ranch in New Mexico, which at 321,703 acres cost $18 million.[410] Purchase of Plum Creek's two million acres would dwarf anything TNC has done.

It has been suggested that the grant lands be acquired at the price specified by the 1870 grant, not more than $2.50 per acre. There is railroad land grant precedent for this, such as the 1916 O&C Railroad revestment, in which Congress compensated the railroad $2.50 per acre. The O&C Railroad claimed this was an unconstitutional "taking" and a violation of due process, since the land was by then worth more than that. The Supreme Court upheld the constitutionality of the revestment and compensation, reasoning that the O&C should not profit from its failure to sell the land as required.[411] Following this precedent in the case of the Northern Pacific grant would lower the price to reacquire Northern Pacific grant land under Plum Creek control from $527 million to about $5 million.

There would likely be two general groups of individuals and organizations which would strenuously object to the purchase of checkerboard lands by the federal government. The first would consist of those who oppose restoring lands to the public domain

---

[408]   AP, Jan. 29, 1992; and AP, April 23, 1992. In early 1993, the House of Representatives passed a bill which authorized acquisition of 80,000 acres north of Yellowstone National Park at a cost of $12 to $20 million. The government would use exchanges or cash to acquire the land from the Blixseth Group which bought the land from Plum Creek in 1992 and which could soon begin cutting the trees. The bill's sponsor, Pat Williams (D-MT), said, "[I]f this legislation isn't enacted we face a public lands disaster on Yellowstone National Park's northern border" (*Seattle Times*, May 23, 1993). Note that this land, which the federal government must acquire to avert a "public lands disaster," was conditionally granted to Northern Pacific "to promote the public interest and welfare. . . ."

[409]   Selcraig, 1990, p.52.

[410]   Selcraig, 1990, p.32.

[411]   See Goetz (1979, pp.75-76, 99-102, 41-45), citing the Chamberlain-Ferris Act, 39 Stat. 218, (1916), and O&C v. United States, 483 U.S. 549, (1917). Another precedent is that when Native American land claims are recognized, the federal government often compensates them using the value of the lands at the time the nineteenth century treaties were signed.

because they would consider it an unfair "taking" of private property (although in this case corporate control derives from repeated violations of Congressional contracts). The second group would consist of those who point to the Northern Pacific's repeated breaches of its contract with Congress, and the violation of public trust. For these people, the appropriate action would be for Congress to exert its oversight authority to protect the public interest as expressly allowed in the law, rather than to continue to reward the Northern Pacific's corporate descendants for their behavior.

(3) Revestment

Arguing against reopening the grant are those who have suggested that the 1941 settlement closed the door on the land grant case.[412] However, under the Constitution of the United States, Congress retains authority to reopen the Northern Pacific grant. This authority was expressly reserved in Section 20 of the 1864 grant, which stated that Congress may at any time "add to, alter, amend, or repeal this act." Further, a review of the 1940 Supreme Court documents and of the 1941 settlement reveals that many important issues were not resolved. The issues which the Supreme Court had expressly reserved for future consideration do not appear in the 1941 settlement with Northern Pacific. Further, the judge who presided over the settlement wrote that "Congress has not authorized this settlement. . . . [The settlement] is not an act of Congress, and is in no way binding on the Congress. . . ."[413]

To address the unresolved issues surrounding the railroad land grants would require that numerous other questions be raised about the "claiming" of the West. These include the decline of forest conditions, the role of timber corporations in the current forest crisis, and the methods by which the West was opened for settlement. Other questions which Congress might wish to consider include:

- What are the continuing obligations between the grant lands and the associated rail transportation system?

---

[412] For example, Cotroneo (1980) and Wilner (1981).
[413] Judge Schwellenbach in U.S. v. Northern Pacific, 41 F. Supp. 283-284 (1941).

- What would be the effects of the land-grant investigation on Burlington Northern's other spin-offs, such as Burlington Resources?[414]

- What would be the status of the more than 13.3 million acres taken from Native American reservations for Northern Pacific use?[415] Would these lands revert to their original inhabitants?

- What would be the effects of a revestment of lands which other corporations, such as Weyerhaeuser, Potlatch, and Boise Cascade, have acquired from the Northern Pacific land grant?

There are numerous precedents for readdressing railroad land grants. For example, Congress in 1916 revested railroad grant lands in western Oregon based on an 1866 railroad grant.[416] Today these lands, the so-called O&C lands, are administered by the U.S. Bureau of Land Management (and figure prominently in the spotted owl debate). Another case occurred in 1890, when Congress culminated 12 years of attempts to revest the Northern Pacific railroad grant lands by revesting two million acres, as well as millions of acres from other grants.[417] A third case is provided by President Coolidge's reopening of the Northern Pacific grant 60 years after the original grant and 34 years after the previous Northern Pacific revestment.[418]

There is increasing national awareness of the crises in the health of the Pacific Northwest's forests and economies. Congressional authority is clear. Congress may at any time exercise its constitutional authority to "add to, alter, amend, or repeal this act."

---

[414]   Plum Creek represents only 4 percent of the assets of the Burlington Northern empire; see footnote 85.

[415]   For example, 30,000 square miles of land were taken from the Blackfoot, the Arikaris, and the Gros Ventre to allow Northern Pacific to pass (Brown, 1978, pp.257-258). See also Cotroneo, 1966, pp. 275-285.

[416]   39 Stat. 218.

[417]   26 Stat. 496.

[418]   43 Stat. 461.

CONCLUSIONS

The intent of our analysis has been to restore to the national debate over forests the central importance of a federal law passed during the Civil War promoting railroad construction in the Western territories.

In 1864 President Lincoln signed a "contract or covenant" (as President Coolidge was to call it in 1924)[419] creating Northern Pacific Company and conditionally granting to it 40 million acres of public land for the purpose of building and maintaining a railroad from Lake Superior to the Pacific Ocean. This was the largest of the nation's railroad land grants. The checkerboard and in-lieu strips covered an area approximately 120 miles wide and 2,000 miles long.

In order to protect the public interest and because of the immensity of the land area involved, Congress explicitly reserved to itself oversight authority in Section 20 of the grant:

> . . . Congress may, at any time, having due regard for
> the rights of said Northern Pacific Railroad Company,
> add to, alter, amend, or repeal this act.

The main line of the Northern Pacific Railroad was eventually completed in 1883. In the 1890s the two main lines serving the northern tier states, Northern Pacific and Great Northern, were effectively combined by J.P. Morgan and James J. Hill to form a

---

[419] *New York Times*, Feb. 26, 1924. For a modern analysis of the contract's problems, see Baldwin, 1981.

railroad monopoly. In 1896 and 1904 the Supreme Court struck down the monopoly. In 1970 the Supreme Court acceeded to the merger. Northern Pacific, Great Northern, Chicago Burlington & Quincy, and other railroads formally became Burlington Northern. In 1988 millions of acres of Northern Pacific grant lands that had been bound to the railroad by J. P. Morgan's long term bonds were stripped away to form Burlington Resources and other spin-off corporations such as Plum Creek.

President Coolidge and Congress in the 1920s concluded that the contract signed by Lincoln had been repeatedly and flagrantly violated by Northern Pacific and its corporate heirs. Major conditions of the grant had not been kept. These obligations included keeping deadlines for railroad financing and completion, auctioning granted lands locally when Northern Pacific failed in 1873 and in 1893, and opening lands to homesteaders within five years of completing the main line in 1883. Indeed, many grant lands were sold in small parcels to settlers as intended by Congress. But millions of acres of railroad land-grant lands, including some of the most valuable public lands in the United States, came under the control of a few financiers and gave rise to unintended corporate empires. Today these land-grant-based corporations exert enormous political and economic influence in the Pacific Northwest and the rest of the nation.

In this manner, the 1864 Northern Pacific railroad land grant became the foundation upon which major timber corporations today base their claims to millions of acres of Pacific Northwest forests. These companies include Weyerhaeuser, Potlatch, Boise Cascade, and Plum Creek.

Land-grant forests have been managed for short-term corporate profits rather than for sustainability. The resulting shortage in the Pacific Northwest timber supply has profound economic and social implications for timber-dependent communities.

The economic and environmental impacts of overcutting are not newly recognized. In 1940 President Roosevelt's Agriculture Secretary Henry Wallace warned the Pacific Northwest against overcutting the forests. Wallace specifically mentioned the checkerboard lands, writing that it is "impossible to work out effective plans for management under these circumstances."[420] Wallace's

---

[420]   Wallace, Aug. 25, 1940.

prophetic warnings went unheeded. Fifty years later, forest liquidation on the checkerboards has cut a swath of destruction from Yellowstone National Park to the Pacific Ocean.

In the checkerboard pattern of intermingling ownership, environmental damage on the land-grant sections also damages adjacent National Forest sections. Forest Service officials are then faced with the choice of violating national environmental protection laws or reducing logging, further reducing timber available for Pacific Northwest mills.

President Bill Clinton hosted a national conference on forests on April 2, 1993, in Portland, Oregon, in which the concept of "ecosystem management" was a central theme. Managing Pacific Northwest forests as ecosystems will be impossible, however, so long as the checkerboard pattern resulting from the 1864 law exists. The checkerboard pattern superimposed on the forests scrambles any coherent policy for millions of acres of Pacific Northwest forests.

Land-grant logs and fiber originally intended to generate capital to build and maintain a railroad are exported overseas, bypassing American mills and opportunities for value-added industries. Weyerhaeuser, a $13 billion timber corporation based largely on Congress's Northern Pacific land grant in the Pacific Northwest, is a major exporter of land-grant logs. Plum Creek, another railroad-based timber company, also exports logs. Plum Creek can export land-grant logs from the Cascades Range to Japan, convert yen to dollars, and use the profits to bid against smaller mills for publicly subsidized timber sales in the National Forests of eastern Washington, Idaho, and Montana.

When log export policies were reformed in 1990, Congress made possible an end to the exporting of logs from state forests and National Forests – but not from forest "ownerships" based on Congress's 1864 Northern Pacific railroad land grant.

Congress's land-grant legacy is alive in the Pacific Northwest and takes the form of log exports, checkerboard forests, unrelenting "public education" campaigns, wealthy lobby groups, and large corporations that wield enormous political and economic influence at the state capitals and in Washington, D.C.

Several options exist to resolve the problems stemming from the overcutting of the Pacific Northwest's land-grant forests. These range from incentives or regulations at the state level to revisiting the fundamental "cooperative" relationship between timber companies and the federal government established in the 1924 Clarke-McNary Act. But, since the forest crisis derives largely from Congress's 1864 Northern Pacific land grant, one compelling option is to reform this law. While Congress can always undertake reform of existing legislation, Congress has explicitly retained for itself oversight of the 1864 Northern Pacific land grant. Section 20 provides that "Congress, may, at any time, having due regard for the rights of said Northern Pacific Railroad Company, add to, alter, amend, or repeal this act."

Congress has already established a record of revesting railroad grant lands. Failure to fulfill contractual obligations has led Congress to take back millions of acres of railroad grant lands and restore them to public ownership. Major revestments or forfeitures occurred in 1890 involving Northern Pacific and other railroad companies and in 1916 involving the O&C lands in western Oregon originally granted in 1866. In 1924 when President Coolidge asked Congress to investigate the Northern Pacific grant, he began an effort that ultimately restored 2.9 million acres to the public domain in 1941, but that left key and troubling issues unresolved.

President Coolidge stated that Congress could take action even though the violations of the contract had occurred many years earlier:

> The defaults of the Northern Pacific were numerous and flagrant, and the supplementary benefits allowed by the Government were many and lavish, but in the absence of action by Congress the courts and the administrative departments were and are without authority to consider the resulting equities, but have been forced to act as though the company had complied with every term of the grant, both in spirit and letter. Congress, as the contracting power in this case, has the power and authority to determine what weight shall be given to such violations of the grant for the purpose of ascertaining whether they have been fairly satisfied to date by the United States. . . . [421]

---

[421] President Coolidge quoting Agriculture Secretary Henry C. Wallace in Coolidge's letter to Senator Lenroot of the Senate Committee on Public Lands, Feb. 21, 1924. President Coolidge's letter is reprinted in full in "Land Grant Inquiry Urged by Coolidge," *New York Times,* Feb. 26, 1924. This letter appears in Appendix 3.

The Congressional investigation in the 1920s ultimately concluded that violations of the law had occurred. That these violations had occurred years earlier did not stop Congress from investigating the abuses of the grant, nor from directing the Department of Justice to take legal action to protect the public interest.

When, in 1929, Congress and President Hoover directed the Justice Department to take legal action against Northern Pacific, they directed that all issues be evaluated and decided by the courts, and that the outcome be reported to Congress by the Attorney General. The lawsuit was filed in 1930 in Spokane. In 1940 the Supreme Court generally decided against the railroad but split on several key issues which were then remanded back to the lower court in Spokane. In 1941 a partial settlement was reached in which Northern Pacific abandoned claims to 2.9 million acres of National Forests. The full and complete accounting directed by Congress of the Northern Pacific land grant breaches never took place.

The 1941 settlement did not close the case on Northern Pacific. In 1981 a Congressional Research Service analysis reinforced the conclusion that Congress can take action to clarify unresolved questions about the grant. Indeed, another law enacted during the nation's frontier period, the 1872 Mining Act, is the focus of reform efforts now underway in Congress. The 1864 grant is an old law, but the mere age of a law does not preclude its reform. In fact, some would argue that because of the age of the law, reform should be encouraged.

The 1864 Northern Pacific railroad land grant is the defining piece of legislation for the Pacific Northwest and is at the core of the American forest crisis. The conditions and intent of the law have been violated, with enormous consequences for Pacific Northwest forests and communities from Yellowstone National Park to the Pacific Ocean.

In 1864, during the Civil War, the forests of the Pacific Northwest had not yet been logged and extended from the Yellowstone and Rocky Mountain Front across parts of the Columbia River Watershed to the Pacific Ocean. Across this same region today, watersheds are unraveling, and the spotted owl, the marbled murrelet, the grizzly bear, many runs of salmon, and other species of flora and fauna have become threatened, endangered, or extinct through the last century of excessive logging.

Today, the timber frontier in America is over. The native forests have been logged from the Atlantic Ocean to the Pacific Ocean. During the past century, millions of acres of public forests in the West conditionally granted by Congress to build and maintain a railroad instead passed into the hands of a few timber companies. The land-grant-based timber companies have overcut the Pacific Northwest, and have been transferring capital out of the region to the American Southeast, Canada, Latin America, Asia, and other "timber frontiers." As happened after the forests of New England and the Great Lakes were cut down, the Pacific Northwest today faces the long-predicted and difficult problems of cutover forests and a timber shortage that is forcing a historic transition for forest-dependent communities in the rural Pacific Northwest.

Congress can take action. Congress can always reform existing legislation. In this case, Congress also retains explicit oversight authority for the grant and "may, at any time, having due regard for the rights of said Northern Pacific Railroad Company, add to, alter, amend, or repeal this act."

Large corporations that have so greatly benefited at public expense will argue that these lands are private and that they were purchased. But, if the defaults on the Congressional contracts were indeed "numerous and flagrant," as President Coolidge asserted in 1924 and as Congress and President Hoover confirmed in 1929, then ownership of millions of acres claimed by Plum Creek, Weyerhaeuser, Potlatch, and Boise Cascade remains in doubt. Rather than private property, this is land from the public domain subject to the obligations of the Northern Pacific railroad land grants and to public and Congressional oversight.

APPENDICES

1864 LAND GRANT (13 STAT. 366)

[Spelling and punctuation as in original]
CHAP. CCXVII. – An Act granting Lands to aid in the Construction of a Railroad and Telegraph Line from Lake Superior to Puget's Sound, on the Pacific Coast, by the Northern Route.

Be it enacted by the Senate and the House of Representatives of the United States of America in Congress assembled, That Richard D. Rice, John A. Poore, Samuel P. Strickland, Samuel C. Fessenden, Charles P. Kimball, Augustine Haines, Edwin R. W. Wiggin, Anson P. Morrill, Samuel J. Anderson, of Maine; Willard Sears, I. S. Withington, Josiah Perham, James M. Becket, A W. Banfield, Abiel Abbott, John Newell, Austin L. Rogers, Nathaniel Greene, jnr., Oliver Frost, John A. Bass, John O. Bresbrey, George Shiverick, Edward Tyler, Filander J. Forristall, Ivory H. Pope, of Massachusetts; George Opdyke, Fairley Holmes, John Huggins, Philander Reed, George Briggs, Chauncey Vibbard, John C. Fremont, of New York; Ephraim Marsh, John P Jackson, jr., of New Jersey; S. M. Felton, John Toy, O. J. Dickey, B. F. Archer. G. W. Cass, J. Edgar Thompson, John A. Green, of Pennsylvania; T. M. Allyn, Moses W. Wilson, Horace Whittaker, Ira Bliss, of Connecticut; Joseph A. Gilmore, Onslo Stearns, E. P. Emerson, Frederick Smyth, William E. Chandler, of New Hampshire; Cyrus Aldrich, H.M. Rice, John McKusick, H. C. Waite, Stephen Miller, of Minnesota; E. A. Chapin, John Gregory Smith, George Merrill, of Vermont; James Y. Smith, William S. Slater, Isaac H. Southwick, Earl P. Mason, of Rhode Island; Seth Fuller, William Kellogg, U. S. Grant, William B. Ogden, William G. Greene, Leonard Sweat, Henry W. Blodgett, Porter Sheldon, of Illinois; J. M. Winchell, Elsworth Cheesebrough, James S. Emery, of Kansas; Richard F. Perkins, Richard Chenery, Samuel Brannan, George Rowland, Henry Platt, of California; William F. Mercer, James W. Brownley, of Virginia; John H. B. Latrobe, W. Prescott Smith, of Maryland; Greenbury Slack, A. J. Boreman, of West Virginia; Thomas E. Bramlette, Frank Shorin, of Kentucky; John Brough, John A. Bingham, Oran Follett, John Gardner, S. S.

L'Hommedieu, Harrison G. Blake, Philo Chamberlain, of Ohio; John A. Duncan, Samuel M. Harrington, of Delaware; Thomas A. Morris, Jesse Williams, of Indiana; Samuel L. Case, Henry L. Hall, David H. Jerome, Thomas D. Gilbert, C. A. Trowbridge, of Michigan; Edward H. Broadhead, Alexander Mitchell, Benjamin Ferguson, Levi Sterling, — Marshal, of Wisconsin; J. C. Ainsworth, Orlando Humason, H. W. Corbett, Henry Failling, of Oregon; J. B. S. Todd, M. K. Armstrong, J. Shaw Gregory, J. Le Berge, of Dakota Territory; John Mullan, Anson G. Henry, S. D. Smith, Charles Terry of Washington Territory; H. W. Starr, Platt Smith, Nixon Denton, William Leighton, B. F. Allen, Reuben Noble, John L. Davies, of Iowa; Willard P. Hall, George R. Smith, H. Gayle King, John C. Sargeant, of Missouri; William H. Wallace, of Idaho Territory; J. H. Lathrop, Henry D. Cooke, H. E. Merrick, of the District of Columbia, and all such other persons who shall or may be associated with them, and their successors, are hereby created and erected into a body corporate and politic, in deed and in law, by the name, style, and title of the "Northern Pacific Railroad Company," and by that name shall have perpetual succession, and shall be able to sue and to be sued, plead and be impleaded, defend and be defended, in all courts of law and equity within the United States, and may make and have a common seal. And said corporation is hereby authorized and empowered to lay out, locate, construct, furnish, maintain, and enjoy a continuous railroad and telegraph line, with the appurtenances, namely, beginning at a point on Lake Superior, in the State of Minnesota or Wisconsin; thence westerly by the most eligible railroad route, as shall be determined by said company, within the territory of the United States, on a line north of the forty-fifth degree of latitude to some point on Puget's Sound, with a branch, via the valley of the Columbia River, to a point at or near Portland, in the State of Oregon, leaving the main trunk line at the most suitable place, not more than three hundred miles from its western terminus; and is hereby vested with all the powers, privileges, and immunities necessary to carry into effect the purposes of this act as herein set forth. The capital stock of said company shall consist of one million shares of one hundred dollars each, which shall in all respects be deemed personal property, and shall be transferable in such manner as the by-laws of said corporation shall provide. The persons herein before named are hereby appointed commissioners, and shall be called the board of commissioners of the "Northern Pacific Railroad Company," and fifteen shall constitu[t]e a quorum for the transaction of business. The first meeting of said board of commissioners shall be held at the Melodion hall, in the city of Boston, at such time as any five commissioners herein named from Massachusetts shall appoint, not more than three months after the passage of this act, notice of which shall be given by them to other commissioners by publishing said notice in at least one daily newspaper in the cities of Boston, New York, Philadelphia, Cincinnati, Milwaukee, and Chicago, once a week at least four weeks previous to the day of the meeting. Said board shall organize by the choice from its number of a president, vice-president, secretary, and treasurer, and they shall require from said treasurer such bonds as may be deemed proper, and may from time to time increase the amount thereof as they may deem proper. The secretary shall be sworn to the faithful performance of his duties, and such oath shall be entered upon the records of the company, signed by him, and the oath verified thereon. The president and secretary of said board shall in like manner call all other meetings, naming the time and place thereof. It shall be the duty of said board of commissioners to open books, or cause books to be opened, at such times, and in such principal cities or other places in the United States, as they, or a quorum of them, shall determine, within six months after the passage of this act, to receive subscriptions to the capital stock of said corporation, and a cash payment of ten per centum on all subscriptions, and to receipt therefor. So soon as twenty thousand shares shall in good faith be subscribed for, and ten dollars per share actually paid into the treasury of the company, the said president and secretary of said board of commissioners shall appoint a time and place for the first meeting of the subscribers to the stock of said company, and shall give notice thereof in at least one newspaper in each state in which subscription books have been opened, at least fifteen days previous to the day of meeting, and such subscribers as shall attend the meeting so called, either in person or by lawful proxy, then and there shall elect by ballot thirteen directors for said corporation; and in such election each share of said capital stock shall entitle the owner thereof to one vote. The president and secretary of the board of commissioners, and, in case of their absence or inability, any two of the officers of said board, shall act as inspectors of said election, and shall certify under their hands the names of the directors elected at said meeting; and the said commissioners, treasurer, and secretary, shall then deliver over to said directors all the properties, subscription books, and other books in their possession, and thereupon the duties of said commissioners, and the officers previously appointed by them, shall cease and determine forever, and thereafter the stockholders shall constitute said body politic and corporate. Annual meetings of the stockholders of the said corporation for the choice of officers (when they are to be chosen) and for the transaction of business shall be holden at such time and place and upon such notice as may be prescribed in the by-laws.

SEC. 2. *And be it further enacted,* That the right of way through the public lands be, and the same is hereby, granted to said "Northern Pacific Railroad Company," its successors and assigns, for the construction of a railroad and telegraph as proposed; and the right, power, and authority is hereby given to said corporation to take from the public lands, adjacent to the line of said road, material of earth, stone, timber, and so forth, for the construction thereof. Said way is granted to said railroad to the extent of two hundred feet in width on each side of said railroad where it may pass through the public domain, including all necessary ground for station buildings, workshops, depots, machine shops, switches, side tracks, turn-tables, and water-stations; and the right of way shall be exempt from taxation within the territories of the United States. The United States shall extinguish, as rapidly as may be consistent with public policy and the welfare of the said Indians, the Indian titles to all lands falling under the operation of this act, and acquired in the donation to the [road] named in this bill.

SEC. 3. *And be it further enacted,* That there be, and hereby is, granted to the "Northern Pacific Railroad Company," its successors and assigns, for the purpose of aiding in the construction of said railroad and telegraph line to the Pacific coast, and to secure the safe and speedy transportation of the mails, troops, munitions of war, and public stores, over the route of said line of railway, every alternate section of public land, not mineral, designated by odd numbers, to the amount of twenty alternate sections per mile, on each side of said railroad line, as said company may adopt, through the territories of the United States, and ten alternate sections of land per mile on each side of said railroad whenever it passes through any state, and whenever on the line thereof, the United States have full title, not reserved, sold, granted, or otherwise appropriated, and free from preemption, or other claims or rights, at the time the line of said road is definitely fixed, and a plat thereof filed in the office of the commissioner of the general land-office; and whenever, prior to said time, any of said sections or parts of sections shall have been granted, sold, reserved, occupied by homestead settlers, or preempted, or otherwise disposed of, other lands shall be selected by said company in lieu thereof, under the direction of the Secretary of the Interior, in alternate sections, and designated by odd numbers, not more than ten miles beyond the limits of said alternate sections: *Provided,* That if said route shall be found upon the line of any other railroad route to aid in the construction of which lands have been heretofore granted by the United States, as far as the routes are upon the same general line, the amount of land heretofore granted shall be deducted from the amount granted by this act: *Provided,* further, That the railroad company receiving the previous grant of land may assign their interest to said "Northern Pacific Railroad Company," or may consolidate, confederate, and associate with said company upon the terms named in the first section of this act: *Provided,* further, That all mineral lands be, and the same are hereby, excluded from the operations of this act, and in lieu thereof a like quantity of unoccupied and unappropriated agricultural lands, in odd numbered sections, nearest to the line of said road may be selected as above *provided*: And *provided, further*, That the word "mineral," when it occurs in this act, shall not be held to include iron or coal: And provided, further, That no money shall be drawn from the treasury of the United States to aid in the construction of the said "Northern Pacific Railroad."

SEC. 4. *And be it further enacted,* That whenever said "Northern Pacific Railroad Company" shall have twenty-five consecutive miles of any portion of said railroad and telegraph line ready for the service contemplated, the President of the United States shall appoint three commissioners to examine the same, and if it shall appear that twenty-five consecutive miles of said road and telegraph line have been completed in a good, substantial, and workmanlike manner, as in all other respects required by this act, the commissioners shall so report to the President of the United States, and patents of lands, as aforesaid, shall be issued to said company, confirming to said company the right and title to said lands, situated opposite to, and coterminous with, said completed section of said road; and, from time to time, whenever twenty-five additional consecutive miles shall have been constructed, completed, and in readiness as aforesaid, and verified by said commissioners to the President of the United States, then patents shall be issued to said company conveying the additional sections of land as aforesaid, and so on as fast as every twenty-five miles of said road is completed as aforesaid: *Provided,* That not more than ten sections of land per mile, as said road shall be completed, shall be conveyed to said company for all that part of said railroad lying east of the western boundary of the State of Minnesota, until the whole of said railroad shall be finished and in good running order, as a first-class railroad, from the place of beginning on Lake Superior to the western boundary of Minnesota: Provided, also, That lands shall not be granted under the provisions of this act on account of any railroad, or part thereof, constructed at the date of the passage of this act.

SEC. 5. *And be it further enacted,* That said Northern Pacific Railroad shall be constructed in a substantial and workmanlike manner, with all the necessary draws, culverts, bridges, viaducts, crossings, turnouts, stations, and watering places, and all other appurtenances, including furniture, and rolling stock, equal in all respects to railroads of the first class, when prepared for business, with rails of the best quality, manufactured from American iron. And a uniform gauge shall be established throughout the entire length of the road. And there shall be constructed a telegraph line, of the most substantial and approved description, to be operated along the entire line: *Provided,* That the said company shall not charge the government higher rates than they do individuals for like transportation and telegraphic service. And it shall be the duty of the Northern Pacific Railroad Company to permit any other railroad which shall be authorized to be built by the United States, or by the legislature of any territory or state in which the same may be situated, to form running connections with it, on fair and equitable terms.

SEC. 6. *And be it further enacted,* That the President of the United States shall cause the lands to be surveyed for forty miles in width on both sides of the entire line of said road, after the general route shall be fixed, and as fast as may be required by the construction of said railroad; and the odd sections of land hereby granted shall not be liable to sale, or entry, or preemption before or after they are surveyed, except by said company, as provided in this act; but the provisions of the act of September, eighteen hundred and forty-one, granting preemption rights, and the acts amendatory thereof, and of the act entitled "An act to secure homesteads to actual settlers on the public domain," approved May twenty, eighteen hundred and sixty-two, shall be, and the same are hereby, extended to all other lands on the line of said road, when surveyed, excepting those hereby granted to said company. And the reserved alternate sections shall not be sold by the government at a price less than two dollars and fifty cents per acre, when offered for sale.

SEC. 7. *And be it further enacted,* That the said "Northern Pacific Railroad Company" be, and is hereby, authorized and empowered to enter upon, purchase, take, and hold any lands or premises that may be necessary and proper for the construction and working of said road, not exceeding in width two hundred feet on each side of the line of its railroad, unless a greater width be required for the purpose of excavation or embankment; and also any lands or premises that may be necessary and proper for turnouts, standing places for cars, depots, station-houses, or any other structures required in the construction and working of said road. And the said company shall have the right to cut and remove trees and other material that might, by falling, encumber its road-bed, though standing or being more than two hundred feet from the line of said road. And in case the owner of such lands or premises and the said company cannot agree as to the value of the premises taken, or to be taken, for the use of said road, the value thereof shall be determined by the appraisal of three disinterested commissioners, who may be appointed, upon application by either party, to any court of record in any of the territories in which the lands or premises to be taken lie; and said commissioners, in their assessment of damages, shall appraise such premises at what would have been the value thereof if the road had not been built. And upon return into court of such appraisement, and upon the payment into the same of the estimated value of the premises taken for the use and benefit of the owner thereof, said premises shall be deemed to be taken by said company, which shall thereby acquire full title to the same for the purposes aforesaid. And either party feeling aggrieved at said appraisement may, within thirty days after the same has been returned into court, file an appeal therefrom, and demand a jury of twelve men to estimate the damage sustained; but such appeal shall not interfere with the rights of said company to enter upon the premises taken, or to do any act necessary and proper in the construction of its road. And said party appealing shall give bonds, with sufficient surety or sureties, for the payment of any cost that may arise upon such appeal; and in case the party appealing does not obtain a verdict, increasing or diminishing, as the case may be, the award of the commissioners, such party shall pay the whole cost incurred by the appellee, as well as his own, and the payment into court, for the use of the owner of said premises taken, of a sum equal to that finally awarded, shall be held to vest in said company the title of said land, and of the right to use and occupy the same for the construction, maintenance, and operation of said road. And in case any of the lands to be taken, as aforesaid, shall be held by any infant, femme covert, non compos, insane person, or persons residing without the territory within which the lands to be taken lie, or persons subjected to any legal disability, the court may appoint a guardian for any party under any disqualification, to appear in proper person, who shall give bonds, with sufficient surety or sureties, for the proper and faithful execution of his trust, and who may represent in court the person disqualified, as aforesaid, from appearing, when the same proceedings shall be had in reference to the appraisement of the premises to be taken for the use of said company, and with the same effect as has been already described; and the title of the company to the lands taken by virtue of this act shall not be affected or impaired by reason of any failure by any guardian to discharge faithfully his trust. And in case any party shall have a right or claim to any land for a term of years, or any interest therein, in possession, reversion, or remainder, the value of any such estate, less than a fee simple, shall be estimated and determined in the manner hereinbefore set forth. And in case it shall be necessary for the company to enter upon any lands which are unoccupied, and of which there is no apparent owner or claimant, it may proceed to take and use the same for the purposes of said railroad, and may institute proceedings, in manner described, for the purpose of ascertaining the value of, and of acquiring title to, the same; but the judge of the court hearing said suit shall determine the kind of notice to be served on such owner or owners, and he may in its discretion appoint an agent or guardian to represent such owner or owners in case of his or their incapacity or non-appearance. But in case no claimant shall appear within six years from the time of the opening of said road across any land, all claims to damages against said company shall be barred.

SEC. 8. *And be it further enacted,* That each and every grant, right, and privilege herein are so made and given to, and accepted by, said Northern Pacific Railroad Company, upon and subject to the following conditions, namely: That the said company shall commence the work on said road within two years from the approval of this act by the President, and shall complete not less than fifty miles per year after the second year, and shall construct, equip, furnish, and complete the whole road by the fourth day of July, anno Domini eighteen hundred and seventy-six.

SEC. 9. *And be it further enacted,* That the United States make the several conditioned grants herein, and that the said Northern Pacific Railroad Company accept the same, upon the further condition that if the said company make any breach of the conditions hereof, and allow the same to continue for upwards of one year, then, in such case, at any time hereafter, the United States, by its congress, may do any and all acts and things which may be needful and necessary to insure a speedy completion of said road.

SEC. 10. *And be it further enacted,* That all people of the United States shall have the right to subscribe to the stock of the Northern Pacific Railroad Company until the whole capital named in this act of incorporation is taken up, by complying with the terms of subscriptions; and no mortgage or construction bonds shall ever be issued by said company on said road, or mortgage, or lien made in any way, except by the consent of the congress of the United States.

SEC. 11. *And be it further enacted,* That said Northern Pacific Railroad, or any part thereof, shall be a post route and a military road, subject to the use of the United States, for postal, military, naval, and all other government service, and also subject to such regulations as congress may impose restricting the charges for such government transportation.

SEC. 12. *And be it further enacted,* That the acceptance of the terms, conditions, and impositions of this act by said Northern Pacific Railroad Company shall be signified in writing under the corporate seal of said company, duly executed pursuant to the direction of its board of directors first had and obtained, which acceptance shall be made within two years after the passage of this act, and not afterwards, and shall be served on the President of the United States.

SEC. 13. *And be it further enacted,* That the directors of said company shall make an annual report of their proceedings and expenditures, verified by the affidavits of the president and at least six of the directors, and they shall, from time to time, fix, determine, and regulate the fares, tolls, and charges to be received and paid for transportation of persons and property on said road, or any part thereof.

SEC. 14. *And be it further enacted,* That the directors chosen in pursuance of the first section of this act, shall, so soon as may be after their election, elect from their own number a president and vice-president; and said board of directors shall, from time to time, and so soon as may be after their election, choose a treasurer and secretary, who shall hold their offices at the will and pleasure of the board of directors. The treasurer and secretary shall give such bonds, with such security as the said board from time to time may require. The secretary shall, before entering upon his duty, be sworn to the faithful discharge thereof, and said oath shall be made a matter of record upon the books of said corporation. No person shall be a director of said company unless he shall be a stockholder, and qualified to vote for directors at the election at which he shall be chosen.

SEC. 15. *And be it further enacted,* That the president, vice-president, and directors shall hold their offices for the period indicated in the by-laws of said company, not exceeding three years, respectively, and until others are chosen in their place, and qualified. In case it shall so happen that an election of directors shall not be made on any day appointed by the by-laws of said company, the corporation shall not for that excuse be deemed to be dissolved, but such election may be holden on any day which shall be appointed by the directors. The directors, of whom seven, including the president, shall be a quorum for the transaction of business, shall have full power to make and prescribe such by-laws, rules, and regulations as they shall deem needful and proper touching the disposition and management of the stock, property, estate, and effects of the company, the transfer of shares, the duties and conduct of their officers and servants touching the election and meeting of the directors, and all matters whatsoever which may appertain to the concerns of said company; and the said board of directors may have full power to fill any vacancy or vacancies that may occur from any cause or causes from time to time in their said board. And the said board of directors shall have power to appoint such engineers, agents, and subordinates as may from time to time be necessary to carry into effect the object of the company, and to do all acts and things touching the location and construction of said road.

SEC. 16. *And be it further enacted,* That it shall be lawful for the directors of said company to require payment of the sum of ten per centum cash assessment upon all subscriptions received of all subscribers, and the balance thereof at such times and in such proportions and on such conditions as they shall deem to be necessary to complete the said road and telegraph line within the time in this act prescribed. Sixty days' previous notice shall be given of the payments required, and of the time and place of payment, by publishing a notice once a week in one daily newspaper in each of the cities of Boston, New York, Philidelphia, and Chicago; and in case any stockholder shall neglect or refuse to pay, in pursuance of such notice, the stock held by such person shall be forfeited absolutely to the use of the company, and also any payment or payments that shall have been made on account thereof, subject to the condition that the board of directors may allow the redemption on such terms as they may prescribe.

SEC. 17. *And be it further enacted,* That the said company is authorized to accept to its own use any grant, donation, loan, power, franchise, aid, or assistance which may be granted to, or conferred upon, said company by the congress of the United States, by the legislature of any state, or by any corporation, person, or persons; and said corporation is authorized to hold and enjoy any such grant, donation, loan, power, franchise, aid, or assistance, to its own use for the purpose aforesaid.

SEC. 18. *And be it further enacted,* That said Northern Pacific Railroad Company shall obtain the consent of the legislature of any state through which any portion of said railroad line may pass, previous to commencing the construction thereof; but said company may have the right to put on engineers and survey the route before obtaining the consent of the legislature.

SEC. 19. *And be it further enacted,* That unless said Northern Pacific Railroad Company shall obtain bona fide subscriptions to the stock of said company to the amount of two millions of dollars, with ten per centum paid within two years after the passage and approval of this act, it shall be null and void.

SEC. 20. *And be it further enacted,* That the better to accomplish the object of this act, namely, to promote the public interest and welfare by the construction of said railroad and telgraph line, and keeping the same in working order, and to secure to the government at all time (but particularily in time of war) the use and benefit of the same for postal, military, and other purposes, congress may, at any time, having due regard for the rights of said Northern Pacific Railroad Company, add to, alter, amend, or repeal this act.

APPROVED, July 2, 1864.

1870 LAND GRANT (16 STAT. 378)

[No. 67.] A Resolution authorizing the Northern Pacific Railroad Company to issue its Bonds for the Construction of its Road and to secure the same by Mortgage, and for other Purposes.

Resolved by the Senate and House of Representatives of the United States of America in Congress assembled, That the Northern Pacific Railroad Company be, and hereby is, authorized to issue its bonds to aid in the construction and equipment of its road, and to secure the same by mortgage on its property of all kinds and descriptions, real, personal, and mixed, including its franchise as a corporation; and, as proof and notice of its legal execution and effectual delivery, said mortgage shall be filed and recorded in the office of the Secretary of the Interior; and also to locate and construct, under the provisions and with the privileges, grants, and duties provided for in its act of incorporation, its main road to some point on Puget Sound, via the valley of the Columbia river, with the right to locate and construct its branch from some convenient point on its main trunk line across the Cascade Mountains to Puget Sound; and in the event of there not being any State or Territory in which said main line or branch may be located, at the time of the final location thereof, the amount of lands per mile granted by Congress to said company, within the limits prescribed by its charter, then said company shall be entitled, under the directions of the Secretary of the Interior, to receive so many sections of land belonging to the United States, and designated by odd numbers, in such State or Territory, within ten miles on each side of said road, beyond the limits prescribed in said charter, as will make up such deficiency, on said main line or branch, except mineral and other lands as excepted in the charter of said company of eighteen hundred and sixty-four, to the amount of the lands that have been granted, sold, reserved, occupied by homestead settlers, pre-empted, or otherwise disposed of subsequent to the passage of the act of July two, eighteen hundred and sixty-four. And that twenty-five miles of said main line between its western terminus and the city of Portland, in the State of Oregon, shall be completed by the first day of January, anno Domini eighteen hundred and seventy-two, and forty miles of the remaining portion thereof each year thereafter, until the whole shall be completed between said points: *Provided,* that all lands hereby granted to said company which shall not be sold or disposed of or remain subject to the mortgage by this act authorized, at the expiration of five years after the completion of the entire road, shall be subject to settlement and preemption like other lands, at a price to be paid to said company not exceeding two dollars and fifty cents per acre; and if the mortgage hereby authorized shall at any time be enforced by foreclosure or other legal proceeding, or the mortgaged lands hereby granted, or any of them, be sold by the trustees to whom such mortgage may be executed, either at its maturity or for any failure or default of said company under the terms thereof, such lands shall be sold at public sale, at places within the States and Territories in which they shall be situate, after not less than sixty days' previous notice, in single sections or subdivisions thereof, to the highest and best bidder: *Provided further,* That in the construction of the said railroad, American iron or steel only shall be used, the same to be manufactured from American ores exclusively.

SEC. 2. *And be it further resolved,* That Congress may at any time alter or amend this joint resolution, having due regard to the rights of said company, and any other parties.

APPROVED, May 31, 1870.

APPENDIX 3

PRESIDENT COOLIDGE'S REQUEST FOR CONGRESSIONAL INVESTIGATION

Reprinted from *The New York Times*, February 26, 1924

LAND GRANT INQUIRY URGED BY COOLIDGE

He Asks Congress to Scrutinize Northern Pacific Railroad's Claims to Forest Areas

---

QUICK ACTION IS SOUGHT

President Wants "Fullest Protection of Public Interests" on 3,000,000 Acres in Dispute.

SUPPORTS WALLACE'S PLEA

Letter to Lenroot Holds Titles Should be Held In Abeyance Pending Investigation

---

Special to The New York Times.

WASHINGTON, Feb. 25. – President Coolidge today urged upon Congress the importance of immediate investigation, with a view to legislation to protect the public interests, into the vast acreage of valuable timber lands within the national forests to which the Northern Pacific Railroad lays claim.

More than 3,000,000 acres are involved, and the President shares the view of Secretary Wallace of the Agriculture Department that it is extremely unfortunate if the forest lands have been lost to the Government "if Congress has the authority to save them under legislation which, in the light of all the law and the facts, would be fair and just to the Northern Pacific Railway Company."

The President called the problem to the attention of Congress in a letter to Chairman Lenroot of the Senate Committee on Public Lands, to whom he explained that the possible loss of public title to these resources arises out of an adjudication of the old Northern Pacific Railroad land grant, which Congress authorized in 1864, and under which 40,000,000 acres was to be awarded to the railroad to enable it to throw its line across the continent.

Attention is invited by the President to a communication from Secretary Wallace questioning the extent to which the railroad may have obtained undue benefits from the grant, and the railroad's compliance with the obligations imposed upon it by the legislation authorizing the land award.

Senator Lenroot was informed that the gross receipts of the Northern Pacific from the sale of lands from the time of the grant to June 30, 1917, amounted to $136,118,533.14. The grants were made for the purpose of aiding the construction of the railroad. According to the information laid before Senator Lenroot by the President, the cost of constructing the railroad did not exceed $70,000,000.

The President's Letter.

The President's letter reads:
The White House.
Washington, Feb. 21, 1924.

My Dear Senator:

I desire to bring to your attention a letter from the Secretary of Agriculture under the date of Feb. 19, 1924, in reference to the claim asserted by the Northern Pacific Railroad to large areas of valuable timber land within the national forests.

The possible loss of public title to these resources, which have been protected and developed for many years at public cost, arises under an adjudication of the land grant made by Congress to the

Northern Pacific Railroad in 1864. It is my understanding that the legislation conveing [sic] this grant of 40,000,000 acres of public land was, in effect, a contract or covenant between the United States and the railroad company, under which mutual obligations, particularly on the part of the Government, have from time to time been reviewed and determined by the Federal courts, but their decisions were confined necessarily and purposely to the immediate issues brought before them. At no time does there appear to have been comprehensive review or determination of the entire transaction, covering the mutual equities and obligations created by the covenant, if the grant to the Northern Pacific Railroad may purposely be so designated.

The statements contained in the letter from the Secretary of Agriculture raise serious questions as to the extent to which the railroad company may have obtained undue benefits from the grant, and also as to the extent of its compliance with the obligations imposed upon it by the legislation which conferred the grant. I believe that these questions should be fully determined before a final settlement of the matter is effected and before further public lands are patented to the company. From the nature of the case, and particularly the broad and varied equities which it involves, it would seem that such a determination and settlement can be made only by the Congress.

The United States has granted lavishly of its public resources to aid the extension of transportation facilities and thereby the economic development of the Western States. No question as to the wisdom of that policy is involved in this issue. Nor is any question involved as to the legal and moral obligation of the Government to discharge in full the contractual obligations, which it assumed for the accomplishment of public benefits. That the legal and equitable claims of the grantee should be fully weighted and safeguarded goes without saying. But it is still more imperative that the interests of the public, both in the possession and conservation of valuable natural resources and the accomplishment of the purposes for which the grant was made, be adequately protected in an equitable settlement of this question.

Reviews Wallace's Investigation

The Secretary of Agriculture, in a letter to me, states further a summary of the facts involved in this matter, as they have been developed through a painstaking investigation. The full record of that investigation has no doubt been placed at your disposal. I quote from the letter of Secretary Wallace, dated Feb. 19, 1924:

"In April, 1921, the Supreme Court rendered a decision (256 U.S. 51) with regard to lands in the indemnity limits of the grant to the Northern Pacific, holding that lands in these limits could not be withdrawn by the United States if they were needed to satisfy the acreage of the grant.

"The tentative adjustment made by the Department of the Interior shows the grant to be deficient some 3,900,000 acres.

"Large areas of national forest lands are within the indemnity limits of the grant. It follows that should the tentative adjustment become final, a large acreage of these national forest lands will pass to the Northern Pacific.

"When this situation became evident, this department, through the Forest Service, began a thorough investigation of the Northern Pacific grants. As a result of this investigation certain representations were made to the Department of the Interior, and on January 24, 1924, I addressed a letter to the Secretary of the Interior and asked him to join with me in sending to Congress a proposed joint resolution directing the Secretary of the Interior to withhold his approval of the adjustment of the Northern Pacific land grants until Congress shall have made a full and complete inquiry into them.

"The Secretary of the Interior complied with this request, and the proposed resolution was sent to Congress and was introduced in the House by the Hon. N. J. Sinnott, chairman of the Committee on Public Lands, and in the Senate by Senator Lenroot.

"As this matter no doubt will come to your attention, if it has not already, I desire to give you a brief statement of the reasons for this action by this department.

"The case in which the Supreme Court (256 U.S. 51) defined the measure of the Northern Pacific grants did not take into consideration, and properly so, many other questions which I believe should be considered by Congress before the case reaches the point where the Northern Pacific may take these national forest lands.

"The defaults of the Northern Pacific were numerous and flagrant, and the supplementary benefits allowed by the Government were many and lavish, but in the absence of action by Congress the courts and the administrative departments were and are without authority to consider the resulting equities, but have been forced to act as though the company had complied with every term of the grant, both in spirit and letter. Congress, as to the contracting power in this case, has the power and authority to determine what weight shall be given to such violation of the grant and such beneficial concessions.

"It alone can inquire into the grants for the purpose of ascertaining whether they have been fairly satisfied to date by the United States, taking into consideration the equitable and other features of the grants that were not before the Supreme Court when it handed down its decision (256 U.S., 51).

"I submit that if the proof is sufficient to show that the Northern Pacific failed to meet the requirements of its agreement, or that the Northern Pacific has already received a greater acreage or greater values than it was equitably entitled to receive, Congress has ample authority to save these national forest lands to the Government.

Land Receipts Exceed Road's Cost

"I believe an investigation by Congress would show:

"1. That the land grants were made for the purpose of aiding in the construction of the railroad. The total gross receipts of the Northern Pacific to June 30, 1917, from the sale of the lands from its grant amounted to $136,118,533.14. The cost of constructing the road did not exceed $70,000,000. The sale of lands has more than paid for the cost of constructing the railroad.

"2. That the Northern Pacific failed to construct 1,507.21 miles of its railroad within the time required by law, thereby rendering the granted lands subject to forfeiture.

"3. That the Northern Pacific failed to dispose of certain of its lands to settlers at not to exceed $2.50 per acre as required by the law. A somewhat similar provision in the Oregon and California grant was held by the Supreme Court to be an enforceable covenant (238 U.S., 393).

"4. That the Northern Pacific failed to dispose of hundreds of thousands of acres of its lands at public sale, as required by law.

"5. That hundreds of thousands of acres of poor land in the Northern Pacific grant were erroneously classified as mineral. This land was turned back to the United States and the railroad acquired mineral indemnity rights therefor,[sic] which were applied in part on more valuable lands in the indemnity limits.

"6. That under a rule of law laid down by the Supreme Court the Northern Pacific has been erroneously allowed 1,500,000 acres too much land in the State of Washington.

"7. That over 500,000 acres of land credited to the Northern Pacific should be deducted because of conflict with the land grant of another road, and the erroneous fixation of the land grant limit lines.

"8. That approximately 640,000 acres of land have been erroneously allowed the Northern Pacific by reason of the Tacoma overlap.

"9. That the Northern Pacific has received approximately 600,000 acres of land to which they were not entitled under their grant in the Wallula overlap.

"10. That the Northern Pacific has been allowed to make over 1,300,000 acres of indemnity selection in its second indemnity belt, whereas these selections should have been confined to the first indemnity belt.

"11. That for lands erroneously patented to the Northern Pacific the Government should be entitled to receive at least what the railroad received from the sale of these lands, instead of $1.25 per acre.

"12. That the Northern Pacific, under the Mount Rainier Park act of March 2, 1899, relinquished to the United States thousands of acres of commercially valueless land, and received therefor [sic] selection privileges applicable to the finest lands they could find in the States of Oregon, Washington, Idaho, Montana, North Dakota, Minnesota, and Wisconsin.

"I am sending with this letter a mimeographed pamphlet, which is in the nature of a brief, dealing with the whole matter. This brief was filed by the Forest Service of this department with the General Land Office on July 12, 1923.

"The resolution which has been introduced in Congress does not attempt to take any land from the Northern Pacific. It merely holds the adjustment of the grant and the issuance of further patents in abeyance until Congress has had an opportunity to make an inquiry into the land grants so that it may pass such legislation as it may deem right and proper.

"It is my opinion that the case is beyond question one for the action of Congress. It would be extremely unfortunate if 3,000,000 acres of National Forest lands should be lost to the United States, if Congress has the authority to save them under legislation, which, in the light of all the law and the facts, would be fair and just to the Northern Pacific Railway Company."

For the reason set forth by the Secretary of Agriculture, I heartily concur in his recommendation that the entire matter should receive the attention of Congress. I therefore urge upon your committee the importance of action as early as possible which shall look to the fullest protection of the public interests herewith concerned. The recital of the facts has deeply interested me, and it is this interest, together with the conviction that a highly important public interest can only be effectively protected by appropriate Congressional action, that prompts me to write you. Most sincerely yours,

CALVIN COOLIDGE.

APPENDIX 4

CORPORATE INTERLOCKS

Terms of Selected Officers and Directors of Anaconda Copper, Boise Cascade (Boise), Burlington Northern (B.N.), Burlington Resources (B. Res.), Great Northern (G.N.), Northern Pacific (N.P.), Potlatch, and Weyerhaeuser Corporations

DIRECTOR	ANA-CONDA	BOISE	B.N.	B.RES.	G.N.	N.P.	POT-LATCH	WEYER-HAEUSER
Anderson (Morgan), Arthur M.						1940-59		
Bell, F.S.		1914-34					1903-36	1910-38
Bell, Laird							1931-50	1934-61
Blunt, Carleton		1944-52						1953-75
Brownell (Asarco), Frances H.						1944-51		
Clapp, A.W.								1930-46
Clapp, E.P.		1924-46					1921-47	1921-46
Clapp, Norton		1946 [H]					1947 [H]	1938-[?]
Clapp, William H.								1981 [pp]
Cook (UP), William S.		1979-91						
Davis, Edwin Weyer.							1931 [H]	1947-53
Davis, Frederick Weyer.		[x]					1976-85	[x]
Davis, W.P.							1949 [H]	
Denkmann, F.C.								1900-29
Drexel, Walter	1978-81		1981-85					
Driscoll, Walter John		[x]	1977-81					1979 [pp]
Fery, John B.		1960 [pp]						
Gardner, Booth								1976-80
Grinstein, Gerald			1985 [pp]	1988-91				
Hauberg, Jr., John H.		[x]					[x]	1958-91
Hill, James J.					[x]	[x]		
Hill, James N.					1907-21			
Ingram, C.H.								1900-06
Ingram, Charles H.								1936-62
Ingram, E. Bronson								1967 [pp]
Irvine, H.H.						1944-46		1902-47
Jewett, George Fred.		1933 [H]				1947-55	1931 [H]	
Jewett, Jr., George F.		[x]					1976-85	
Laird, A.W.							1911-31	
Laird, William H.								1900-10
Little, George R.		1929-50					1929-52	1938-53
Love, Ben			1985 [?]	1988				
McClure, James A.		1990 [pp]						
Menk, Louis			1970-82			1966-70		
Morgan Jr., J.P.						1907-20		
Musser, C.R.		1923-50					1903 [H]	1919-50
Musser, John M.		1943 [H]						1950-[?]
Musser, Peter M.								1900-19
Musser, R. Drew		1941 [H]					1903 [H]	
Musser, William		1914-33						
O'Leary, Thomas			1982 [?]	1988 [pp]				
Parrish, John B.		1979-92	1981-83	1983 [?]				
Pascoe, John J.		1960					1976-85	
Piasecki, Vivian							[?]-[pp]	
Ray (GN Iron Ore), Philip L.					[?]	1940-62		
Reed (Simpson), William G.						1956-68		
Reimers, Fred W.							1931 [H]	1929-58
Rockefeller, James S.						1962-68		
Rosenberry, Walter Sam							1931-32	
Rosenberry Jr, Walter Sam		1944-50						
Ruckelshaus, William D.					1987-88			1976 [pp]
Shrontz (Boeing), Frank A.		1989 [pp]						
Thatcher, F.H.		1914-29					1903-21	1909-21
Thompson, G.W.	1979-83		1983-88	1988-90				
Titcomb, E.R.		1960-88						
Titcomb, Jon. R.								1962 [?]
Titcomb, John W.							1952 [H]	

DIRECTOR	ANA-CONDA	BOISE	B.N.	B.RES.	G.N.	N.P.	POT-LATCH	WEYER-HAEUSER
Turrish, Henry	1914-24					1903-27		
Weyerhaeuser, C. Davis		1941 [H]					1947 [H]	1953-79
Weyerhaeuser, C.A.		1927-30				1903-30	1928-30	
Weyerhaeuser I, Frederick	[x]			[x]			1909-14	1900-14
Weyerhaeuser II, Frederick E.		1914-41			1916-32			1906-45
Weyerhaeuser III, Frederick K.							1931-52	1946-65
Weyerhaeuser III, Frederick		[x]					1947 [H]	[x]
Weyerhaeuser IV, Frederick T.							1930-52	
Weyerhaeuser, Frederick T.							1976-85	
Weyerhaeuser, George H.		[x]						1960 [pp]
Weyerhaeuser I, J.P.		1916-35					1909-36	1913-35
Weyerhaeuser II, J.P.							1930-52	1933-56
Weyerhaeuser III, J.P.								1957-60
Weyerhaeuser, R.M.						1926-46	1932-46	1935-46
Weyerhaeuser, William T.							1990-92	
Wilson, Robert B.				1969-81			1966-88	
Wilson (Boeing), T.A.								1983 [pp]
Wood, Donald	1979-81		1981-83					

This chart understates the ties between the various corporations in several important ways. The dates given are inclusive and approximate; in other words, some directors' terms are longer than indicated here. The chart shows directors and executive officers only. It does not show ownership overlaps, such as shareholders in common. This is a complicated but powerful and significant source of overlap, especially for Potlatch and Weyerhaeuser. In addition, there are ties of blood: the Davis, Driscoll, Jewett, Pascoe, Piasecki, Rosenberry, Titcomb, and Weyerhaeuser families have intermarried. The Denkmann, Laird-Norton-Clapp-Bell, and Musser families have also maintained business ties (see Hidy, Hill and Nevins, 1963; and Twining, 1985, for a family tree). This chart is also not comprehensive in regards to companies; several hundred corporations have been combined into eight columns for clarity. For example, Burlington Resources here includes Burlington Environmental, Burlington Resources, Chempro, Ecos, El Paso, Glacier Park, Meridian Minerals and Meridian Oil, and Plum Creek Timber. Finally, only significant, representative directors have been included. A full list would run into many hundreds of names and go back to the 1864 incorporation of Northern Pacific.

Dates with [pp] indicate director as of the 1992 Annual Report.
Dates with [?] indicate term ended, at time unknown.
Dates with [x] indicate possible directorship, but date unknown.
Dates with [H] indicate still shown in Hidy, Hill, and Nevins (1963).
The numbers after the "Frederick" Weyerhaeusers indicate generation.

SOURCES: Annual Reports of the various corporations; Hidy, Hill, and Nevins, 1963, pp.658-665; and Twining, 1985, pp.382-383.

APPENDIX 5

CHRONOLOGY

1864   Northern Pacific land grant is signed by Abraham Lincoln (July 2, 1864, Ch. 217, 13 Stat. 365).

1864   *Man and Nature* is released by George Perkins Marsh. This book will explode the frontier myths of superabundance and the inexhaustibility of nature.

1866 & 1868 Northern Pacific deadlines to begin construction are extended by Congress.

1869   Central Pacific and Union Pacific railroads are joined by a golden spike ceremony in Promontory, Utah. This completes the nation's first "transcontinental," based on the 1862 Pacific Railway Act.

1870   Northern Pacific land grant is amended; additional land is granted and the sale of bonds is authorized (Joint Resolution 67 of May 31, 1870, 16 Stat. 378).

1870-71   Jay Cooke, financier of the Civil War, sells $80 million worth of Northern Pacific bonds.

1870   Northern Pacific construction begins at Duluth, Minnesota, and Kalama, Washington.

1873   The U.S. General Land Office accuses Northern Pacific attorney Hazard Stevens, the son of the Governor of Washington Territory, of stealing logs. Northern Pacific fires him. (Ficken, 1987; Steen, 1969.)

1873   Northern Pacific completes construction from Duluth, Minnesota to Bismarck, South Dakota and from Kalama, Washington to Tacoma, Washington.

1873 The failure of Northern Pacific precipitates the depression of 1873. Construction stops. Grant lands are not sold at local auction.

1874 Windom Senate Committee on railroad abuses.

1874 Granger legislation passes in Iowa and Wisconsin; the Supreme Court upholds them in 1876 (Munn v. Illinois, 94 U.S. 114).

1875 Northern Pacific reorganizes after its 1873 failure, but fails to sell grant lands as required (U.S. Bureau of Corporations, 1913-14, Part I, p. 235).

1876 U.S. Supreme Court rules that breaches of land grants do not automatically return land to government; Congressional action is required (Schulenberg v. Harriman, 21 Wallace 44).

1876 George Armstrong Custer, who has guarded railroad survey and construction crews for several years, is killed in the Battle of the Little Bighorn (Welch and Stekler, 1994).

1876 Dr. Franklin B. Hough convinces Congress to fund a study of forest problems. Dr. Hough's work helps establish the U.S. Forest Service and the National Forest System.

1877 Railroad treatment of workers erupts in strikes and riots across the U.S. in what was later called "The Year of Violence."

1880s Northern Pacific and its Northwestern Improvement Company subsidiary indicted for poaching timber from public land in Washington (Steen, 1969, pp.46-47).

1880s-90s Northern Pacific begins coal mining in Montana (Malone, Roeder, and Lang, 1991, pp.337-338).

1880 Northern Pacific reaches the Yellowstone River in Montana.

1880-81 Henry Villard gains control of Northern Pacific (Hedges, 1930).

1881 Northern Pacific Dakota Territory branch lines are completed.

1882   Northern Pacific holds 7.7 million acres in Washington Territory, including two million acres of commercial timberland (Ficken, 1987, p.45).

1882   Northern Pacific reaches Big Horn River, and completes line from Wallula to Lake Pend d'Oreille.

1883   Northern Pacific completes transcontinental mainline at Gold Creek, Montana, on September 8; the last spike (the same steel spike used to begin construction at Carleton, Minnesota, in 1870) is driven by Henry Villard and former U.S. President Grant (Yenne, 1981, p.38). Construction was originally to have begun in 1866 and be completed in 1876.

1883   Northern Pacific completes construction from Wallula to Tacoma, Washington and Portland, Oregon.

1884   Villard resigns as president of Northern Pacific because of increasing bond debt and fall in stock value.

1886   Cullom Senate Committee on railroad abuses leads to the Interstate Commerce Act.

1887   The Interstate Commerce Act makes railroads the first regulated industry.

1887-88   Northern Pacific crosses Cascades.

1887   Northern Pacific sells 80,000 acres in Washington to the St. Paul & Tacoma Lumber Co., associated with James J. Hill and Frederick Weyerhaeuser.

1889   Sherman Anti-Trust Act passes.

1889-90   Territories become states: North Dakota, South Dakota, Montana, Idaho, and Washington.

1890   Popular resentment against railroad land grants leads to the general forfeiture statute (26 Stat. 496), in which Northern

Pacific forfeits two million acres along the Columbia River (Ellis, 1946).

1890 Weyerhaeuser buys 212,722 acres in eight Minnesota counties from the Northern Pacific railroad. By 1922 Weyerhaeuser's Pine Tree Lumber Company has paid stockholders $11.5 million, but forfeited cutover lands to avoid paying taxes. (Hidy, Hill, and Nevins, 1963, pp.148-149.)

1891 Congress passes the Forest Reserve Act, giving presidents the power to proclaim Forest Reserves (later called National Forests).

1893 Northern Pacific, now composed of 54 railroads, goes bankrupt again. Reorganized in 1896. Grant lands are not legitimately sold at local auction.

1894 Coxey's Army of the Unemployed breaks into the Northern Pacific's Butte, Montana roundhouse and commandeers a train (Schwantes, 1985; and White, 1984).

1894 U.S. Supreme Court rules that Northern Pacific is not entitled to any lands upon which minerals other than coal and iron were found prior to patenting (Barden v. Northern Pacific, 154 U.S. 288, 1894).

1894 Hill and Morgan combine the Northern Pacific and Great Northern Railroads.

1896 Minnesota and the U.S. Supreme Court hold the merger of Northern Pacific and Great Northern to be an illegal combination of "competing" corporations (Pearsall v. Great Northern, 161 U.S. 646). Hill's and Morgan's response is to create joint ownership by individuals, instead of by a corporation.

1896 Morgan refinances Northern Pacific with 100- and 150-year bonds. Morgan's bonds use grant land as collateral; this lien on the development of the land won't be removed until 1988.

1896-1900 Northern Pacific continues branch line construction.

1897 Under threat of foreclosure, Northern Pacific offers Morgan all its lands for $1.75 million.

1897 Congress specifies how the Forest Reserves are to be managed in the Pettigrew Amendment to the Sundry Civil Appropriations Bill, also termed the 1897 Organic Act (Steen, 1991, pp. 34-37).

1897-99 Mt. Rainier Forest Reserve of 2.5 million acres is established. Northern Pacific trades rock and glaciers for nearly half a million acres of timberlands in Oregon, Washington, Idaho, North Dakota, Minnesota, and Wisconsin. (U.S. Bureau of Corporations, 1913-1914, Part 1, pp.237-239.)

1899 Northern Pacific sells 900,000 acres in Washington to Weyerhaeuser for $6.50 per acre. In 1912 the U.S. Bureau of Corporations estimates the purchase price to have been ten cents per thousand board feet for some 17 billion board feet. (Ficken, 1987; and Hidy, Hill, and Nevins, 1963.)

1901 Northern Pacific and GN acquire 97 percent of the Chicago Burlington & Quincy Railroad and create the Northern Securities holding company (Holbrook, 1955, p. 144).

1903 Weyerhaeuser and associates incorporate Potlatch.

1904 U.S. Supreme Court again rules that the combination of Northern Pacific and Great Northern, now called Northern Securities, is a monopoly in violation of the Sherman Anti-Trust Act, and orders it dissolved (Northern Securities v. U.S., 193 U.S. 197). The formal separation of the companies is accomplished by giving the stockholders of each railroad shares in the other company and by putting a wall down the center of their office.

1905 Transfer Act passes. Responsibility of Forest Reserves (renamed National Forests) transferred from the Interior

Department to the Department of Agriculture, Bureau of Forestry (renamed Forest Service). (Pinchot, 1947, pp.256-7.)

1906   Great Northern leases iron ore lands in the Minnesota Mesabi Range to U.S. Steel (Holbrook, 1955, p.146).

1906   Northern Pacific selects indemnity lands withdrawn for Gallatin National Forest: the U.S. sues when Northern Pacific refuses to return them (United States v. Northern Pacific, 256 U.S. 51, 1921).

1907   Northern Pacific sells a million acres of Montana forestland to Anaconda Copper. In 1972 Anaconda sells 670,000 acres of this land to Champion International. In 1993 the land becomes part of a huge land sale to Plum Creek. (Schwennesen, 1993; U.S. Bureau of Corporations, 1913-14, Part I, pp. 234, 241.)

1907   President Teddy Roosevelt establishes 32 new National Forests protecting 17 million acres to "prevent the continued absorption of forest areas by syndicates" (Pinchot, 1947, pp. 299-301; *Spokesman-Review*, 1907).

1908   Roosevelt hosts the White House Conference on Conservation, which promotes conservation as the natural resource policy of American government (*Spokesman-Review*, 1908).

1910   Glacier National Park bill passed, with lobbying by James J. Hill, who later builds the Glacier Park and Many Glacier Hotels (opened in 1913 and 1915). Great Northern subsidiary Glacier Park Co. runs the park concession until 1961. (Yenne, 1991, pp. 80-82.)

1910   Yale gives James J. Hill an honorary Doctor of Law degree. Harvard Business School later names a professorship after Hill.

1913   Weyerhaeuser incorporates Boise Payette.

1913-14   The U.S. Bureau of Corporations' "The Lumber Industry" report shows the three largest holders of timber to be Northern

Pacific Railroad, Southern Pacific Railroad, and Weyerhaeuser; the three are estimated to hold 11 percent of all timber in the country.

1915   Three million acres of Oregon & California Railroad land are revested (O&C v. U.S., 238 U.S. 393, 1915).

1916   James J. Hill dies; he is replaced on the Great Northern board of directors by F.E. Weyerhaeuser.

1921   Supreme Court rules Northern Pacific is entitled to select lands within National Forests if none other are available (U.S. v. Northern Pacific, 256 U.S. 51).

1924   President Coolidge asks Senator Lenroot (Senate Committee on Public Lands) for comprehensive review of the Northern Pacific grant (*New York Times*, Feb. 26, 1924); Congress tells the Dept. of Interior to withhold approval of Northern Pacific land grant adjustments and patents until Congressional inquiry.

1927   Northern Pacific hits the $100 million mark in net grant land sales revenues; the railroad cost $70 million to build (Mercer, 1986, p.200; and *New York Times*, Feb. 26, 1924).

1924-28   Northern Pacific Land Grant Hearings before the House Committee on Public Lands (1924); the Senate Committee on Public Lands and Surveys (1924); and the Joint Committee on Investigation of Northern Pacific Railroad Land Grants (1925-28). Five thousand of pages of testimony submitted. The U.S. Attorney General states Congress can declare the land grant forfeited and should have the issue submitted for judicial resolution. (U.S. Congress, 1924-28, Part 13.)

1930   The U.S. Attorney General files suit in Spokane against Northern Pacific, seeking $50 million and removal of 3.9 million acres from the land grant (*New York Times*, Aug. 1, 1930).

1931   Potlatch is joined with Clearwater and Rutledge Timber Companies.

1940   Supreme Court rules in U.S. v. Northern Pacific (311 U.S. 317), generally deciding in favor of United States against Northern Pacific, remanding the case back to federal district court in Spokane.

1941   Northern Pacific proposes a settlement in which it would relinquish further land or compensation claims and agree to pay the U.S. $300,000, and in return the U.S. would discharge its various claims against Northern Pacific. The Secretaries of Agriculture and the Interior accept, and the settlement is approved by the court and the Attorney General (U.S. v. NP, 41 F. Supp. 287). Congress does not authorize this settlement.

1957   Boise Payette is joined with Cascade Lumber to form Boise Cascade.

1960   Multiple Use - Sustained Yield Act passes, supplanting the 1897 Organic Act.

1970   U.S. Supreme Court upholds the merger of Northern Pacific, Great Northern, and Chicago, Burlington & Quincy into the Burlington Northern (U.S. v ICC, 396 U.S. 491).

1970 & 1977   Interstate Commerce Commission reviews of railroad holding companies conclude that nonrail business is bad for railroads, national transportation, and defense; that railroad dividends have gone to nonrail subsidiaries; that railroads are used to obtain credit without compensation; and that holding company expenses are billed to railroads. The 1977 study stated that the "financial strength of Burlington Northern is due in large measure to the existence and development of its nonrailway assets" (U.S. Interstate Commerce Commission, 1977, p. 51).

1975   U.S. Department of Interior cites Northern Pacific with possible breach of grant, but claims it has no authority or duty to conduct review of land grants or to force railroads to comply with settlement and preemption, claiming Congress has sole authority (Applegate, 1979).

1976 National Forest Management Act passes, supplanting the 1960 Multiple Use - Sustained Yield Act and, in turn, the 1897 Organic Act.

1980 Staggers Act deregulates railroads.

1981 BN reorganizes as a holding company and the corporate headquarters is moved from St. Paul to Seattle.

1983 BN acquires El Paso Natural Gas company in a hostile takeover (Gilbert et al v. El Paso; and Gelobter et al v. Bressler).

1988 The lien on J.P. Morgan's 1896 land grant bonds is broken by settlement, allowing those lands to be spun off and developed (Rievman v. BN, 118 F.R.D. 29, S.D.N.Y., 1987).

1988 Burlington Resources is formed as a holding company for BN's natural resource operations.

1988 Burlington Resources subsidiary Meridian Minerals announces that three million ounces of gold have been found at Beartrack near Salmon, Idaho.

1989 Burlington Resources spins off Plum Creek Timber.

1990 Because of environmental abuses, U.S. Representative Rod Chandler (R-WA) calls Plum Creek "the Darth Vader of the state of Washington" (Farney, June 18, 1990).

1990-92 Trillium Corporation of Bellingham, Washington buys tens of thousands of acres of real estate in 12 states and two Canadian provinces from Burlington Resources subsidiary Glacier Park (Tapperson, 1992).

1992 Twenty-two percent of Burlington Resources's shareholders vote for a resolution requiring the company to prepare a report on its reactions to the Valdez Principles of environmental corporate responsibility; this is the first time more than 20 percent of any corporation's shareholders have approved a "social proxy" issue other than South Africa (Cogan, 1992, p.53). Weyerhaeuser management also rejects endorsing the Principles in 1992 and 1993.

1992 Burlington Resources spins off El Paso Natural Gas.

1992 Plum Creek sells two sawmills and 164,000 acres in Gallatin and Park counties, Montana, to Tim Blixseth of Portland and McDougal Brothers of Dexter, Oregon (AP, April 23, 1992).

1992 New joint ventures are announced to exploit Montana coal: Burlington Resources' Meridian Minerals, Arch Mineral, Ashland Oil, Hunt Industries, Sumitomo, and Mitsui. The rest of the coal properties are spun off into a limited partnership (Great Northern Properties), including coal committed to Western Energy's Rosebud mine and Peabody's Big Sky mine (Dow Jones, July 22, 1992 and Oct. 28, 1992).

1992 Plum Creek admits breaking federal and state election laws by attaching political slogans and anti-wilderness literature to employees' paychecks in Flathead Valley, Montana. Leaflets warn Plum Creek employees they could lose their jobs if they do not attend an anti-wilderness rally in September. Plum Creek is fined the maximum $1,000 (Simonsen, 1992; and *High Country News*, Feb. 22, 1993).

1992 SPO Partners, a small group of investors, acquires control of Plum Creek Timber.

1992 Standard & Poor's lowers Burlington Northern's credit ratings, because of its "aggressively leveraged capital structure related to the spin-off of resources properties without a divestiture of the debt assumed to acquire and develop those properties" (Dow Jones, Nov. 18, 1992).

1992 Burlington Northern Chairman Gerald Grinstein is elected chairman of the Association of American Railroads.

1993 Burlington Resources spins off natural gas properties in New Mexico.

1993   Plum Creek purchases 867,000 acres of western Montana timberland from Champion International, which had purchased it from Anaconda Copper in 1972, which had purchased it from Northern Pacific in 1907 (Devlin, Aug. 1, 1993; and Dow Jones, July 19, and Nov. 2, 1993).

BIBLIOGRAPHY

Adams, Paul W. and Henry A. Froelich
1981   *Compaction of forest soils.* Corvallis, Oregon: Pacific Northwest Extension Service. 12 pp.

Adams, Darius M., Kristine C. Jackson, and Richard W. Haynes
1988   Production, consumption, and prices of softwood products in North America: regional time series data, 1950 to 1985. *Resource Bulletin PNW-RB-151.* Portland, Oregon: U.S. Forest Service, Pacific Northwest Research Station, Jan. 1988. 49 pp.

AFPI (American Forest Products Industries)
1965   *Government land acquisition: a summary of land acquisition by federal, state and local governments up to 1964.* Montana edition. Washington, D.C.: American Forest Products Industries. 31 pp.

Anderson, H. Michael and Jeffrey T. Olson
1991   *Federal forests and the economic base of the Pacific Northwest: a study of regional transitions.* Washington, D.C.: The Wilderness Society, Sept. 1991. 119 pp.

Andrews, Mea
1982   Williams wants BN to still pay for land grants. *Missoulian,* Sept. 12, 1982. Reprinted in *Transitions,* March 1992, p.27.

Anez, Bob
1988   EQC says no to forest practices law. *Missoulian,* Dec. 10, 1988. Reprinted in *Transitions,* July 1992, pp.34-35.
1989   Governor to industry: mend fences. *Missoulian,* Aug. 15, 1989.

AP (Associated Press)
1987   Congressman may try to block road by Plum Creek in Gallatin. *Post Register* (Idaho Falls), Sept. 13, 1987.

1988   Timber companies overcut own land, eye public forests. *Spokesman-Review,* Oct. 17, 1988. Reprinted in *Transitions,* Dec. 1990, pp.4-5.

1989   How state jobs rely on exports. *Seattle Post-Intelligencer,* March 10, 1989, p.C1.

1989   Oregonians vote against export of logs. *Spokesman-Review,* June 28, 1989.

1989   Weyerhaeuser opposes effort to ban log exports. *Lewiston Tribune,* Aug. 25, 1989. Reprinted in *Transitions,* Dec. 1989, p.5.

1989   Investigator claims he lacks backing to stop illegal log exports. *Lewiston Tribune,* Oct. 22, 1989. Reprinted in *Transitions,* Dec. 1989, p.7.

1990   Private timberlands overcut, officials say. *Spokesman-Review,* April 14, 1990. Reprinted in *Transitions,* June 1990, p.6.

1990   Boise Cascade denies timber industry tried to cut water funds. *Times-News* (Twin Falls, Idaho), April 25, 1990. Reprinted in *Transitions,* Nov. 1990, p.6; and July 1992, p.30.

1990   Weyerhaeuser to stop exporting Oregon logs. *Seattle Daily Journal of Commerce,* Nov. 28, 1990.

1990   McClure leaves Senate for Boise Cascade. *Lewiston Tribune,* Dec. 14, 1990.

1991   Timber lobby cuts down proposed regulations [Washington State HB 1823]. *Spokesman-Review,* March 6, 1991. Reprinted in *Transitions,* March 1991, p.4.

1991   Governor praises logging efforts. *Seattle Daily Journal of Commerce,* Aug. 29, 1991.

1991   Champion International puts Montana mills and timberlands up for sale. *Seattle Daily Journal of Commerce,* Sept. 25, 1991, p.5.

1992   Plum Creek breaks off talks with Conservancy. *Missoulian,* Jan. 29, 1992.

1992   Timber land sold to firm in Oregon: deal lamented by conservation activists. *Post-Register* (Idaho Falls, Idaho), April 23, 1992. Reprinted in *Transitions,* April 1992, p.13.

1992   Forest Service chief disputes NASA photos of Northwest logging. *Coeur d'Alene Press*, June 17, 1992.
1993   Senate seeks to ban some log exports. *Seattle Post-Intelligencer*, June 18, 1993, p.C3.

APA (American Plywood Association)
1991   *Geographical analysis of structural panel shipments: 4th quarter 1990, inland region.* Tacoma, Washington: American Plywood Association.

Applegate, Rick
1979   An unintended empire: a case study of rail land holdings. Pages 100-240 in: *Additions to the National Wilderness Preservation System, hearings before the Subcomm. on Public Lands of the Comm. on Interior and Insular Affairs, House of Representatives,* 96th Congress, 1st Session on H.R. 3928, Held in Washington, D.C. on Sept. 17, 1979 . . . and Oversight on Land Ownership in the Beaverhead and Gallatin National Forests, Hearing Held in Bozeman, Montana, Oct. 4, 1979. Serial No. 96-11, Part IV.

Appleman, Roy E.
1939   Timber empire from the public domain. *Mississippi Valley Historical Review* 26: 193-208, Sept. 1939. Also published in Gates, 1979.

Baldwin, Pamela
1981   *A legal analysis of the land grants of the Northern Pacific Railroad.* American Law Division, Congressional Research Service, Library of Congress, Oct. 19, 1981. 40 pp.

Bechtold, Timothy M.
1991   *Now vs. forever: the conflict between business and forestry in the management of Plum Creek timberlands in Montana.* M.S. thesis. Missoula: University of Montana.

Benson, Robert E. et al.
  1985   Cost of managing nontimber resources when harvesting timber in the Northern Rockies. *Research Paper INT-351.* Ogden, Utah: U.S. Forest Service, Intermountain Research Station. 78 pp.
  1987   Idaho's forest resources. *Resource Bulletin INT-39.* Ogden, Utah: U.S. Forest Service, Intermountain Research Station, July 1987. 114 pp.

Bloomberg Business News
  1993   Burlington Resources shifting its focus. *Seattle Times,* March 2, 1993, p.F8.

Blumenthal, Les
  1991   Forest fallout: industry changes, not owl, blamed. *Tacoma News Tribune,* Aug. 18, 1991.

Brazil, Eric
  1989   Export of logs is undercutting 'timber capital': economic forces reworking fabric of town's industry. *San Francisco Examiner and Chronicle,* April 30, 1989.

Brown, Dee
  1978   *Hear that lonesome whistle blow: railroads in the West.* New York: Bantam Books. 309 pp.

Burlington Resources
  1988   *Prospectus for 20 million shares common stock.* Filed with the U.S. Securities and Exchange Commission on June 2, 1988.
  1988   *Amendment No. 2 to Form S-1 registration statement containing a prospectus for the sale of 20 million shares of common stock.* Filed with the U.S. Securities and Exchange on July 7, 1988. 88 pp. plus appendices.

Burns, Conrad
  1990   Letter to U.S. Forest Service Chief Dale Robertson, Sept. 10, 1990. Reprinted in *Transitions,* Dec. 1990, p.11.

Cameron, Mindy
1991   Nature Conservancy decides to mix it up [Glacier Park
        CEO Chris Bayley on Nature Conservancy national board].
        Seattle Times, May 19, 1991.

Cedarholm C.J. and L.M. Reid
1987   Impact of forest management on coho salmon
        (*Oncorhynchus kisutch*) populations of the Clearwater
        River, Washington: a project summary. Pages 372-391 in:
        *Streamside Management: Forestry and Fishery
        Interactions.* Contribution No. 57. Seattle: UW College of
        Forest Resources.

Chernow, Ron
1990   *The house of Morgan: an American banking dynasty and
        the rise of modern finance.* New York: Atlantic Monthly
        Press. 812 pp.

Christner, J. and R.D. Harr
1982   Peak streamflows from the transient snow zone, western
        Cascades, Oregon. Presented at the *Western Snow
        Conference;* Reno, Nevada; April 20, 1982.

Cogan, Douglas G.
1992   Shareholders press environmental issues. *Directors &
        Boards,* Summer 1992, pp. 53-57.

Collins, Dennis C. and Roger C. Conner
1991   Forest statistics for land outside National Forests in
        northwestern Montana, 1989. *Resource Bulletin INT-73.*
        Ogden, Utah: U.S. Forest Service, Intermountain Research
        Station, Aug. 1991.

Connelly, Joel
1989   Senators push Grays Harbor port project. *Seattle Post-
        Intelligencer,* April 5, 1989, p.B2.
1989   Packwood proposal to contain stiff fines for log
        'substitution.' *Seattle Post-Intelligencer,* April 11, 1989

Cotroneo, Ross Ralph
1966   *The history of the Northern Pacific land grant, 1900-1952*. Ph.D. dissertation. Moscow: University of Idaho. Reprinted in 1967 by Arno Press, New York. 468 pp.
1980   United States v. Northern Pacific Railway Company: the final settlement of the land grant case, 1924-1941. *Pacific Northwest Quarterly* 71(3): 107-111, July 1980.

Council on Economic Priorities
1992   [Environmental profiles of Boise Cascade, Champion International, Plum Creek, Potlatch, and Weyerhaeuser]. New York: CEP.

Cox, John H.
1937   *Organizations of the lumber industry in the Pacific Northwest, 1889-1914*. Ph.D. dissertation. Seattle: University of Washington, Dept. of History.

Craig, Larry
1991   Letter to U.S. Forest Service Chief Dale Robertson, May 23, 1991. Reprinted in *Transitions,* Aug. 1991, p.8.

Crain, James R.
1992   Testimony presented to the Subcommittee on Forests, Family Farms, and Energy of the House Agricultural Committee on H.R. 4980, the National Forest Health Act of 1992, by James R. Crane, Vice President of Public Lands, California Forestry Association, Sacramento, July 1, 1992. 2 pp.

Creedy, John A.
1983   Why a Congressional investigation of the rail land grants. *ICC Practitioners' Journal* 50(2):156-162, Jan./Feb. 1983.

Daniels, Orville
1991   Dear Concerned Citizen letter, from forest supervisor of the Lolo National Forest, Sept. 22, 1991. Reprinted in *Transitions,* Dec. 1991, pp.32-33.

de Yonge, John
  1989   159 firms petition U.S. to bar log exports from state lands. *Seattle Post-Intelligencer,* July 24, 1989. Reprinted in *Transitions,* Dec. 1989, p.4.

Devlin, Sherry
  1990   The rough cut of competition: Montana's timber industry faces a future with limits. *Missoulian,* Jan. 14, 1990. Reprinted in *Transitions,* June 1990, pp.8-9.
  1991   USFS suspends some timber sales: supervisor says overcutting makes some areas off-limits to logging. *Missoulian,* Jan. 24, 1991. Reprinted in *Transitions,* May 1992, p.31.
  1991   Foresters cut off the cutting: Buck Creek drainage can't take any more. *Missoulian,* Sept. 4, 1991. Reprinted in *Transitions,* May 1992, p.30.
  1991   Lolo Forest slashes timber cut: industry condemns "arrogant decision." *Missoulian,* Sept. 13, 1991. Reprinted in *Transitions,* Dec. 1991, pp.33-34.
  1991   Forest supervisors get warning. *Missoulian,* Sept. 17, 1991. Reprinted in *Transitions,* Dec. 1991, pp.33-34.
  1991   Plum Creek plan draws fire: company decides to log "critical" elk corridor near Seeley Lake. *Missoulian,* Oct. 3, 1991. Reprinted in *Transitions,* April 1992, p.17.
  1991   Wood wars: industry appeals reduction in Lolo timber-sale program. *Missoulian,* Oct. 31, 1991. Reprinted in *Transitions,* May 1992, p.33.
  1993   The empire strikes back: Plum Creek takes off "Darth Vader" mask. *Missoulian,* Aug. 1, 1993, pp.A1, A10.

DFPI (Directory of the Forest Products Industry)
  1992   *1992-93 directory of the forest products industry.* San Francisco: Miller Freeman.

Dictionary of American Portraits
  1967   *Dictionary of American portraits.* New York: Dover.

Dietrich, William (Bill)
1989   Clear-cuts closer to home: timber cutting sets off widening debate, fresh calls for new regulations. *Seattle Times,* July 13, 1989, pp.A1,A8.
1992   *The final forest: the battle for the last great trees of the Pacific Northwest.* New York: Simon & Schuster. 303 pp.

Dorfman, John R.
1991   Heard on the street: quick recipe for Potlatch potluck: mix hope with takeover talk, add 31 percent to stock price. *Wall Street Journal,* May 28, 1991, p.C2.

Dunn, Marvin
1980   The family office: coordinating mechanism of the ruling class. Pages 17-45 in: *Power Structure Research,* edited by G. William Domhoff. Beverly Hills, California: Sage Publications.

Durbin, Kathie
1990   Forest Service called 'out of control.' *Oregonian,* Jan. 7, 1990.
1990   Politics helped delay NW timber plans. *Oregonian,* Oct. 15, 1990.

Durbin, Kathie and Paul Koberstein
1990   Forests in distress. Series of articles in the *Oregonian,* republished as a special edition on Oct. 15, 1990.

Egan, Timothy
1989   Roslyn journal: where have all the forests gone? *New York Times,* Feb. 15, 1989. Reprinted in *Transitions,* April 1992, p.33.
1990   Forest Service abusing role, dissidents say. *New York Times,* March 4, 1990.
1991   Forest supervisors say politicians are asking them to cut too much. *New York Times,* Sept. 16, 1991. Reprinted in *Transitions,* Dec. 1991, pp.8-9.
1992   Space photos show forests in Pacific Northwest are in peril, scientists say. *New York Times,* June 11, 1992.

Ehrenfeld, David
    1978   *The arrogance of humanism.* New York: Oxford University
            Press. 286 pp.

El Paso Natural Gas Co.
    1992   *Prospectus, May 22, 1992.* Filed with the U.S. Securities
            and Exchange Commission.

Ellefson, Paul V. and Robert N. Stone
    1984   *U.S. wood-based industry: industrial organization and
            performance.* New York: Praeger. 479 pp.

Ellis, David Maldwyn
    1946   The forfeiture of railroad land grants, 1867-1894.
            Mississippi Valley Historical Review 33(1): 27-60, June
            1946.

Epes, James
    1992   Burlington's Glacier Park prepares to close its doors.
            Puget Sound Business Journal, May 8, 1992, p.16.

Fairbanks, Richard
    1992   To mimic nature: new forestry in the Northwest. *Inner
            Voice* 4(4):10-11, July/Aug. 1992.

Fairweather, Hanford W.
    1919   The Northern Pacific Railroad and some of its history.
            Washington Historical Quarterly 10: 95-101, 1919.

Farney, Dennis
    1990   Unkindest cut?: timber firm stirs ire felling forests faster
            than they regenerate; Burlington Northern spinoff clear-
            cuts ancient stands granted by Abe Lincoln; spooked by
            corporate raiders. *Wall Street Journal,* June 18, 1990,
            p.A1. Reprinted in *Transitions,* April 1992, pp.5,7.

Ficken, Robert E.
    1987   *The forested land: a history of lumbering in western
            Washington.* Seattle: University of Washington Press.
            324 pp.

Flora, Donald F.
    1990   Timber exports: winners and losers. *Forest Watch* 10(11):
            9-12,22-25, 1990.

Flora, Donald F. and Wendy J. McGinnis
    1992   Effects of new export rules, a spotted owl plan, and
            recession on timber prices and shipments from the Douglas-
            fir region. *Research Paper PNW-RP-445.* Portland,
            Oregon: U.S. Forest Service, Pacific Northwest Research
            Station, May 1992. 16 pp.

Flowers, Patrick J., James E. Brickell, Alan W. Green, et al.
    1987   Montana's timber supply: an inquiry into possible futures.
            Resource Bulletin INT-40. Ogden, Utah: U.S. Forest
            Service, Intermountain Research Station, March 1987.

Forest Watch
    1986   Weyerhaeuser: a family empire. *Forest Watch,* May 1986,
            pp.6-11. (Originally published in the *Union Register* of
            the Lumber, Production, and Industrial Workers Union.)

Franklin, Jerry F.
    1989   Toward a new forestry. *American Forests,* Nov./Dec.
            1989, pp.37-43.

Frissell, Christopher
    1991   *Water quality, fisheries and aquatic biodiversity under
            two alternative forest management scenarios for the west-
            side federal lands of Washington, Oregon, and northern
            California.* A report prepared for the Wilderness Society.

Gahr, William E.
    1990   *Administration of the federal ban on exports of unprocessed
            federal timber.* Statement before the Subcommittee on
            National Parks and Public Lands, March 20, 1990 (GAO/
            T-RCED-90-51); and before the Subcommittee on Forests,
            Family Farms, and Energy, May 8, 1990 (US GAO/T-
            RCED-90-77). Washington, D.C.: U.S. General
            Accounting Office. 13 pp.

Garrity, Michael T.
1992   Cutting down trees and jobs in Montana. *Forest Watch* 12(8): 22-25, March 1992.

Gast, William R., Donald W. Scott, Craig Schmitt, et al.
1991   *Blue Mountains forest health report: new perspectives in forest health.* U.S. Forest Service, Malheur, Umatilla, and Wallowa Whitman National Forests, April 1991.

Gates, Paul W.
1968   *History of Public Land Law development.* Written for the Public Land Law Review Commission, Washington, D.C., Nov. 1968.

Gillie, John
1990   Tax breaks add to timber profits. *Tacoma Morning News Tribune,* May 27, 1990. Reprinted in *Transitions,* May 1992, p.39.

Glaspell, Kate Eldridge
1941   Incidents in the life of a pioneer. *North Dakota Historical Quarterly,* pp.187-188, 1941.

Goetz, James H.
1979   *The feasibility of legal and/or legislative recourse to remedy violations of the provisions of the Northern Pacific land grant.* Memo to Rick Applegate, Director, Center for Balanced Transportation. Bozeman, Montana: Goetz & Madden, Feb. 5, 1979. 114 pp.

Gorte, Ross
1991   Log export restrictions. *CRS Report for Congress 91-365 ENR.* Washington, D.C.: Congressional Research Service, Library of Congress, April 22, 1991. 4 pp.
1992   Letter to John Osborn of the Inland Empire Public Lands Council, Oct. 1, 1992. Washington, D.C.: Congressional Research Service, Library of Congress.

Green, Mark J. et al.
1972   *The closed enterprise system: Ralph Nader's study group report on antitrust enforcement.* New York: Bantam Books. 488 pp.

Green, Alan W., Renee A. O'Brien, and James C. Schaefer
1985   Montana's forests. *Resource Bulletin INT-38.* Ogden, Utah: U.S. Forest Service, Intermountain Research Station. 70 pp.

Grier, Charles C. et al.
1989   Productivity of forests of the United States and its relation to soil and site factors and management practices: a review. *General Technical Report PNW-GTR-222.* Portland, Oregon: U.S. Forest Service, Pacific Northwest Research Station, March 1989. 51 pp.

Grosse, Daniel J.
1989   *Effectiveness of forestry best management practices in protecting fish resources of two national forests in western Washington.* EPA 910/9-89-008. Seattle: U.S. Environmental Protection Agency, Region 10, July 1989. 39 pp.

Grunbaum, Rami
1992   Burlington may sell its Plum Creek timber stake to Bass. *Puget Sound Business Journal,* Oct. 2-Oct. 8, 1992.

Hadley, Jane
1988   State timber sales may defer to spotted owl. *Seattle Post-Intelligencer,* March 2, 1988, pp. B1, B5.

Harman, John W.
1989   *Administration of the federal ban on exports of unprocessed federal timber.* Statement submitted to the Subcommittee on International Finance and Monetary Policy, Committee on Banking, U.S. Senate, Nov. 7, 1989. U.S. GAO/T-RCED-90-8. Washington, D.C.: U.S. General Accounting Office. 13 pp.

Harris, Larry D.
1984   *The fragmented forest: island biogeography theory and the preservation of biotic diversity.* Chicago: University of Chicago Press. 211 pp.

Healy, Tim
1990   Log-export ban called threat. *Seattle Times,* Oct. 11, 1990.

Hedges, James Blaine
1930   *Henry Villard and the railways of the Northwest.* New Haven: Yale University Press. 224 pp.

Heede, Burchard H.
1991   Response of a stream in disequilibrium to timber harvest. *Environmental Management* 15(2): 251-255, 1991.

Henry, Robert S.
1945   The railroad land grant legend in American history texts. *Mississippi Valley Historical Review* 32(2): 171-194, Sept. 1945.

Hicks, Lorin L.
1991   Plum Creek Timber Company's new forestry experiments: lessons learned and future directions. *Forest Perspectives,* 1(3): 9-10, Fall 1991.

Hidy, Ralph W., Muriel E. Hidy, and Roy V. Scott, with Don L. Hofsommer
1988   *The Great Northern Railway: a history.* Boston: Harvard Business School Press. 360pp.

Hidy, Ralph W., Frank Ernest Hill, and Allan Nevins
1963   *Timber and men: the Weyerhaeuser story.* New York: Macmillan. 704pp.

High Country News
1987   A Forest Service timber study draws fire. *High Country News,* April 27, 1987.
1993   Timber company fined for political fliers. *High Country News,* Feb. 22, 1993.

Hines, Judith A.
1987   Log export restrictions of the western states and British Columbia. *General Technical Report PNW-GTR-208.* Portland, Oregon: U.S. Forest Service, Pacific Northwest Research Station. 13 pp.

Hinson, Joe
1990   Letter to Idaho State Representative Dean Haagenson, Feb. 2, 1990. Reprinted in *Transitions,* July 1992, p.31.

Holbrook, Stewart H.
1947   *The story of American railroads.* New York: Crown. 468 pp.
1953   *The age of the moguls.* New York: Doubleday & Co. 373 pp.
1955   *James J. Hill: a great life in brief.* New York: Alfred A. Knopf. 205 pp.

Hoover's Handbook of American Business
1992   Austin, Texas: The Reference Press. 630 pp.

Hough, Franklin B.
1874   *Cultivation of timber and the preservation of forests.* Report No. 259, 43rd Cong., 1st sess., March 17, 1874. Reprinted in *Transitions,* Sept. 1991, pp.24-27.
1878-84. *Report on forestry.* U.S. Forest Service. Washington, D.C.: U.S. Government Printing Office. Approx. 650 pages in 4 volumes.

Idaho Conservation League
1992   The endless effort: chronology of Idaho's anti-degradation water quality issue. *ICL News,* April 1992. Reprinted in *Transitions,* July 1992, p.32.

Ingram
1991   Memorandum from Oregon Department of Fish & Wildlife on road closure in the Suislaw National Forest.

Isaacson, Allen
1992   Personal communication with author Derrick Jensen.

Jackson, Stanley
1983   *J.P. Morgan: a biography.* New York: Stein and Day. 332 pp.

Jensen International
1991   *Opportunities for value-added wood products.* Prepared for the Washington State Department of Trade and Economic Development, by Jensen International, Alexandria, Virginia, April 1991. 5 volumes.

Jermane, W.E.
1907   Weyerhaeuser in with Hill on lumber: timberman is director of the Great Northern, and railroad magnate is owner of large forests; heads of the newly formed trust will soon control both the raw and the finished products. *Seattle Daily Times,* Sept. 3, 1907.

Jones, Daniel P.
1984   Reagan appointee to forest post formerly a timber firm lawyer. *Denver Post,* Oct. 21, 1984.

Jones, Robert Bradley
1973   *One by one: a documentary narrative based upon the history of the Oregon & California Railroad land grant in the State of Oregon.* A condensed preliminary presentation originally published by the *Source Magazine, Inc.*; reprinted as a public service by ABS, 3434 North Pacific Highway, Medford, Oregon, 1990. 172 pp.

Jones, Steve
1981   Road built in wilderness study area: groups go to court over BN construction. *Missoulian,* Dec. 5, 1981. Reprinted in *Transitions,* May 1992, pp.36-37.

Journal of Commerce
1991   Weyerhaeuser considering Soviet venture. Published in
the *Spokesman-Review,* Sept. 19, 1991, and reprinted in
Transitions, July 1992, p.85.

Kappesser, Gary
1991   *A procedure for evaluating risk of increasing peak flows
from rain on snow events by creating openings in the
forest canopy.* U.S. Forest Service, Idaho Panhandle
National Forest, March 1991.

Keegan, Charles E. and Paul E. Polzin
1987   Trends in the wood and paper products industry. *Journal
of Forestry* 85(11): 31-36, Nov. 1987.

Keegan, Charles E., Timothy P. Jackson, and Maxine C. Johnson
1982   *Idaho's forest products industry: a descriptive analysis
1979.* Missoula: University of Montana Bureau of Business
and Economic Research and the U.S. Forest Service
Intermountain Forest and Range Experiment Station, Sept.
1982. 98 pp.
1983   *Montana's forest products industry: a descriptive analysis
1981.* Missoula: University of Montana Bureau of Business
and Economic Research and the U.S. Forest Service
Intermountain Forest and Range Experiment Station, Aug.
1983. 85 pp.

Keegan, Charles E., K. Jefferson Martin, Maxine C. Johnson, and
Dwane D. Van Hooser
1988   *Idaho's forest products industry: a descriptive analysis
1985.* Missoula: University of Montana Bureau of Business
and Economic Research and the U.S. Forest Service
Intermountain Forest and Range Experiment Station, Jan.
1988. 90 pp.

Keegan, Charles E., Larry D. Swanson, Daniel P. Wichman, and
    Dwane D. Van Hooser
1990   *Montana's forest products industry: a descriptive analysis
    1969-88.* Missoula: University of Montana Bureau of
    Business and Economic Research, Dec. 1990. 52 pp.

Klahn, Jim
1989   Pinched NW mills watch logs head overseas. *Spokesman-
    Review,* May 31, 1989.

Klahr, Trish
1992   Anti-degradation: was it worth it? *Idaho Conservation
    League News,* April 1992. Reprinted in *Transitions,* July
    1992, p.33.

Knudsen, Karen and Jeffrey St. Clair
1991   Reforming the 25 percent fund. *Forest Watch,* Sept. 13,
    1991.

Koberstein, Paul
1990   Private forests face critical log shortages. *Oregonian,* Oct.
    15, 1990. Part of the "Forests in Distress" series by Kathie
    Durbin and Paul Koberstein.

Layton, Mike
1988   Don't blame the spotted owl for crowded classrooms in
    schools. *Seattle Post-Intelligencer,* Jan. 7, 1988.
1988   A tale about owls, the legislature and UW. *Seattle Post-
    Intelligencer,* Feb. 4, 1988.

LeVere, William P., Terry L. Raettig, and Alan W. Green
1987   *A report on Idaho's timber supply.* U.S. Forest Service,
    Feb. 1987.

Lewiston Tribune
1987   Timber study unveiled: Forest Service is optimistic in
    outlook for northern Idaho. Feb. 10, 1987.
1987   Idaho's Jim McClure puts democracy on hold. Editorial,
    Sept. 25, 1987. Reprinted in *Transitions,* Oct. 1987, p.2.

1988   Andrus, McClure stick to plan. Oct. 31, 1988.

Lien, Carsten
1991   *Olympic battleground: the power politics of timber preservation.* San Francisco: Sierra Club Books. 434 pp.

Loftus, Bill
1992   Timber company fights decision: Plum Creek Co. denied easy access to area near Powell. *Lewiston Tribune,* Jan. 4, 1992. Reprinted in *Transitions,* May 1992, pp.34-35.
1992   Ousted forester breaks silence. *Lewiston Tribune,* May 8, 1992.

Long, James
1993   Of grants and greed. *Oregonian,* May 23, 1993, pp.A1,A16-A17. Reprinted in *Transitions,* Dec. 1993, pp.10-17.

Lyon, L. Jack
1984   Field tests of elk/timber coordination guidelines. *Research Paper INT-325.* Ogden, Utah: U.S. Forest Service, Intermountain Research Station.

MacColl, E. Kimbark
1993   Keynote speech at Presidential Forest Conference, April 2, 1993.

Malone, Michael P., Richard B. Roeder, and William L. Lang
1991   *Montana: a history of two centuries.* Revised edition. Seattle: University of Washington Press. 466 pp.

Manning, Richard
1988   Logging outstrips growth: observers warn of effects on environment, industry. *Missoulian,* Oct. 16, 1988. Reprinted in *Transitions,* May 1992, pp.26-27.
1988   Skids fuel furor. *Missoulian,* Oct. 19, 1988. Reprinted in *Transitions,* Dec. 1988, pp.12-13.
1988   Logging spurs regulatory move. *Missoulian,* Oct. 21, 1988. Reprinted in *Transitions,* Dec. 1988, pp.18-19.

1989   Log exports continue to expand; report: Plum Creek a major shipper. *Missoulian,* Feb. 26, 1989. Reprinted in *Transitions,* May 1990, p.12.
1989   Faced with litigation, company halts Lindbergh logging. *Missoulian,* Aug. 12, 1989. Reprinted in *Transitions,* April 1992, p.19.
1991   *The last stand: logging, journalism, and the case for humility.* Salt Lake City: Gibbs Smith Peregrine Books. pp.179.

Marple's Business Newsletter
1988   Breaking up: Burlington Northern Inc., June 22, 1988, pp.2-3.

Marsh, George Perkins
1864   *Man and nature: or physical geography as modified by human action.* New York: Scribner's Sons. Republished by the Harvard University Press in 1965. 472 pp.

Martin, Albro
1976   *James J. Hill and the opening of the Northwest.* New York: Oxford University Press. 679 pp.

Maser, Chris
1988   *The redesigned forest.* San Pedro, California: R. & E. Miles. 234 pp.
1991   Of metallic wood borers, hypogeous fungi, and pooparoonies. *Wild Earth* 1(3): 26-30, Fall 1991.

McCarthy, John
1986   Timber interests. *Lewiston Tribune,* Nov. 3, 1986.

McClure, James
1987   Letter to U.S. Forest Service Chief Dale Robertson. Published in the *Lewiston Tribune,* Sept. 25, 1987. Reprinted in *Transitions,* Oct. 1987, pp.3-5.
1989   Quote on spotted owls reprinted in *Transitions,* June 1989, p.2.

McCoy, Charles
  1992   Corporate focus: Potlatch Corp. expects earnings recovery
         to take root; concern's timber holdings largely immune to
         spotted owl controversy. *Wall Street Journal*, April 13,
         1992, p.B4.

McDermott, Jim
  1993   *News from Congressman Jim McDermott: budget bill
         includes $270 million for timber counties.* Washington,
         D.C.: Office of U.S. Rep. Jim McDermott (D-WA). Six
         page press release, Aug. 6, 1993.

Mercer, Lloyd J.
  1982   *Railroads and the land grant policy: a study in government
         intervention.* New York: Academic Press. 268 pp.

Miller, Dean
  1994   Ex-Idaho senators find home inside the beltway. *The
         Spokesman-Review*, Sept. 25, 1994, pp. A1, A10. Reprinted
         in *Transitions*, Sept. / Oct. 1994, pp. 31-34.

Miller, Freeman
  1991   *Forest Industries 1991-92 North American Factbook.* San
         Francisco: Miller Freeman Publications. Annual.

Miller, Michael W.
  1987   Corporate giant fights the specter of robber baron:
         Burlington Northern seeks to remove J.P. Morgan's liens
         on its lands. *Wall Street Journal*, May 20, 1987. Reprinted
         in *Transitions*, July 1990, pp.8-9.

Minnegerode, Meade
  1927   *Certain rich men.* New York: G.P. Putnam's Sons. 210 pp.

Morgan, Murray
  1982   *The mill on the boot: the story of the St. Paul & Tacoma
         Lumber Company.* Seattle: University of Washington
         Press. 286 pp.

Morrison, Peter
1990   *Ancient forests on the Olympic National Forest: analysis from a historical and landscape perspective.* Washington, D.C.: The Wilderness Society. 21 pp.

Moskowitz, Milton, Michael Katz, and Robert Levering
1980   *Everybody's business: an almanac.* San Francisco: Harper & Row. 916 pp.

Moskowitz, Milton, Robert Levering, and Michael Katz
1990   *Everybody's business: a field guide to the 400 leading companies in America.* New York: Doubleday Currency. 732 pp.

Myers, Carol
1992   U.S. Forest Service Region One Lands and Minerals staff member. Personal communication with George Draffan, July 31, 1992.

Nehlsen, Willa, Jack E. Williams, and James A. Lichatowich
1991   Pacific salmon at the crossroads: stocks at risk from California, Oregon, Idaho, and Washington. *Fisheries* 16(2): 4-21, March/April 1991.

New York Times
1901   Disaster and ruin in falling market; panic without a parallel in Wall Street; losses untold millions; Northern Pacific corner broken too late to save "shorts"; bankers' relief pool; $19,500,000 subscribed when money mounted to sixty per cent—Northern Pacific stock went to 1000—general extent of the crash greater than on Black Friday. May 10, 1901. Reprinted in *Transitions,* Feb. 1992, p.39.
1916   Succeeds James J. Hill: F.E. Weyerhaeuser elected a director of the Gt. Northern Railway. Oct. 14, 1916. p.11.
1924   Land grant inquiry urged by Coolidge: he asks Congress to scrutinize Northern Pacific Railroad's claims to forest areas. Feb. 26, 1924. Reprinted in *Transitions,* March 1992, pp.5-7.

1924   Land inquiry scored by Northern Pacific: President Donnelly calls it an attempt to circumvent the courts through Congress. Feb. 27, 1924. Reprinted in *Transitions,* March 1992, p.9.

1929   Hoover signs bill taking land grant: Northern Pacific area of 2,800,000 acres removed to be forest reserve; railroad allowed to sue; this will determine whether compensation is due, ending a long dispute. June 26, 1929. Reprinted in *Transitions,* March 1992, p.13.

1930   Government sues Northern Pacific; government action filed at Spokane involves $50,000,000 in land. Reprinted in *Transitions*, March 1992, pp. 15.

1990   Some blame disaster on clearcuts, development. Published by the *Lewiston Tribune*, Nov. 27, 1990. Reprinted in *Transitions,* June 1991, p.5.

Newmark, W.D.

1985   Legal and biotic boundaries of western North American national parks: a problem of congruence. *Biological Conservation* 33: 197-208, 1985.

Nogaki, Sylvia Weiland

1990   In the land of logs: ban on exports seen as no panacea for small, troubled sawmills in the Northwest. *Seattle Times,* June 11, 1990, pp.B1, B8.

1991   Timber companies urged to make finished products. *Seattle Times,* June 27, 1991.

Norman, James R.

1992   Divide and prosper. *Forbes,* March 30, 1992, pp.45-46.

Norse, Elliott A.

1990   *Ancient forests of the Pacific Northwest.* Washington, D.C.: The Wilderness Society/Island Press, 1990. 327 pp.

Northern Pacific

1883   *New and correct map of the lines of the Northern Pacific Railroad and Oregon Railway and Navigation Co.* Nov., 1883.

Noss, Reed
    1992   *Biodiversity in the Blue Mountains: a framework for monitoring and assessment.* Produced for distribution at the 1992 Blue Mountains Biodiversity Conference; Whitman College, Walla Walla, Washington; May 26-29, 1992. 14 pp.
    1992   Personal communication with author Derrick Jensen, Dec. 1992.

Oberholtzer, Ellis P.
    1907   *Jay Cooke: financier of the Civil War.* Philadelphia: George Jacobs and Co. 2 vols.

O'Brien, Renee A. and Dennis C. Collins
    1991   Forest statistics for land outside National forests in west-central Montana, 1989. *Resource Bulletin INT-72.* Ogden, Utah: U.S. Forest Service, Intermountain Research Station, June 1991.

O'Connor, Richard
    1953   *Iron wheels and broken men.* New York: G.P. Putnam's Sons. 380 pp.

Osborn, John
    1991   Statement at USDA hearings on securing sourcing area applications pursuant to the Forest Resources Conservation and Shortages Relief Act of 1990, held on April 16, 1991, at Seattle, Washington.

Palmer, Victor
    1991   Findings of fact and conclusions of law, and memorandum in support of application by Plum Creek Management Company; hearings on securing area applications pursuant to the Forest Resources Conservation and Shortage and Relief Act of 1990. FSSAA Docket No. 91-1, et al. Victor W. Palmer, Chief Administrative Law Judge, for the U.S. Dept. of Agriculture. 19 pp. [The document is printed on the letterhead of the Perkins Coie law firm's Bellevue, Washington office].

Pinchot, Gifford
    1919   The lines are drawn. *Journal of Forestry* 17(8):899-900, 1919.
    1947   *Breaking new ground.* Washington, D.C.: Island Press. 522 pp.

Plum Creek Timber Co.
    1988   *Financial portrait.* Company brochure, circa 1988.
    1989   *Prospectus: Plum Creek Timber Company, L.P., 12,350,000 depository units representing limited partner interests.* Subject to completion, dated May 3, 1989. 114 pp. plus appendices. Filed with the U.S. Securities and Exchange Commission.

Polzin, P.E.
    1990   *The spatial distribution of wood products industries.* Missoula: University of Montana, School of Business Administration.

Power, Tom
    1992   The timber employment impact of the Northern Rockies Ecosystem Protection Act in Idaho. Summarized in three parts in *The Networker: News from the Wild Rockies Bioregion,* 1992. Missoula, Montana: Alliance for the Wild Rockies.

Puter, Stephen and Horace Stevens
    1908   *Looters of the Public Domain.* Portland, Oregon: The Portland Printing House Publishers.

Pyle, Joseph G.
    1968   *The life of James J. Hill.* Gloucester, Massachusets: Peter Smith. 2 vols. Originally published in 1916-1917.

Ramsey, Bruce
    1987   A conversation with David Leland: forest firm's 'boom and gloom' times. *Seattle Post-Intelligencer,* Nov. 1987.
    1989   Plum Creek timber restructures to chop taxes. *Seattle Post-Intelligencer,* April 17, 1989, p.B6.

Rhodes, Jon and Richard Jones
1991   *Riparian area management: current management situation and the need for improved riparian management.* Memorandum to Clearwater National Forest Supervisor in reply to 2526, Dec. 19, 1991, regarding Headwaters Stream Forest Plan Appeal.

Rice, Raymond H.
1980   A perspective on the cumulative effects of logging on streamflow and sedimentation. Pages 36-46 in: *Proceedings of the Edgebrook Conference,* Berkeley, California; July 2-3, 1980. University of California, Division of Agricultural Science. Special Publication No. 3268.

Richards, Bill
1992   Silver lining: owls, of all things, help Weyerhaeuser to cash in on timber. *Wall Street Journal,* June 24, 1992.

Richards, Paul
1989   Illegal log exports threaten mill jobs. *Idaho Statesman,* Nov. 25, 1989. Reprinted in *Transitions,* Dec. 1989, p.6.

Riley, James
1992   Written statement, for the record, of James Riley, Executive Vice President, Intermountain Forest Industry Association and the National Forest Products Association, before the Forest, Family Farms & Energy Subcommittee of the Agriculture Committee of the United States House of Representative, July 1, 1992. 6 pp.

Robbins, William G.
1988   *Hard times in paradise: Coos Bay, Oregon, 1850-1986.* Seattle: University of Washington Press. 194 pp.

Roberts, Paul
1990   Boyle calls his lawyer: the lands commissioner says the trust fund has been raided by the governor. *Seattle Weekly,* Sept. 19, 1990.

Robertson, Lance
1990   Timber gets unlikely critic. *Register Guard (Eugene, Oregon)*, Nov. 22, 1990.

Robinson, Gordon
1988   *The forest and the trees: a guide to excellent forestry.* Washington, D.C.: Island Press. 257 pp.

Roederer, Tom
1989   Access to public land: the Keystone dialogue project. *Transactions of the 54th North American Wildlife and Natural Resources Conference,* pp.162-163.

Root, Thomas E.
1987   *Railroad land grants from canals to transcontinentals: 1808 to 1941.* Natural Resources Law Section Monograph Series No. 4. Section of Natural Resources Law, American Bar Association, and The National Energy Law & Policy Institute, University of Tulsa College of Law. 121 pp.

Sacks, Terry
1988   Critics: BN monopoly hurts Montana. *Bozeman Daily Chronicle.* Reprinted in *Spokesman-Review,* Feb. 2, 1988; and in *Transitions,* Feb. 1992, pp.18, 20-21.

Sadler, Russell
1987   Forest production up, jobs down. *Oregonian,* July 26, 1987.

Salo, Sarah Jenkins
1945   *Timber concentration in the Pacific Northwest: with special reference to the timber holdings of the Northern Pacific Railroad and the Weyerhaeuser Timber Company.* Ph.D. dissertation. New York: Columbia University.

Sample, V. Alaric and Dennis C. LeMaster
1992   *Assessing the employment impacts of proposed measures to protect the northern spotted owl.* American Forestry Association, Forest Policy Center. 23 pp.

Scates, Shelby

    1987   Matter of log exports rolls into big Senate campaign issue. *Seattle Post-Intelligencer,* Nov. 12, 1987.

    1989   Bird-brained state doesn't give a hoot about log exports. *Seattle Post-Intelligencer,* March 5, 1989.

    1989   Set-asides, log exports have land commissioner up a tree. *Seattle Post-Intelligencer,* April 18, 1989.

    1989   Oregon puts up roadblock to stop federal log exports. *Seattle Post-Intelligencer,* Jan. 22, 1989.

    1989   Peninsula timber workers await word on log exports. *Seattle Post-Intelligencer,* Dec. 21, 1989.

    1990   NW "Keystone Kops" chase anti-log export bandwagon. *Seattle Post-Intelligencer,* May 8, 1990.

    1990   Irony in probable lineup for raw-log export showdown. *Seattle Post-Intelligencer,* Sept. 25, 1990.

    1991   Gorton shifts on log export limits. *Seattle Post-Intelligencer,* Sept. 29, 1991.

    1992   Log exporters on the welfare dole. *Seattle Post-Intelligencer,* June 21, 1992.

Schaefer, David

    1990   Adams backs ban on export of private timber. *Seattle Times,* June 15, 1990, p.A11.

    1990   Ban on exporting of private logs would face fight. *Seattle Times,* Aug. 31, 1990.

    1992   Bill would end tax break for exporting raw logs. *Seattle Times,* June 2, 1992, p.B4.

    1992   Log-export ban to be expanded. *Seattle Times,* Sept. 18, 1992.

Schowalter, T.D.

    1991   Roles of insects and diseases in sustaining forests. Pages 262-267 in: *Proceedings of the Silviculture Forest Genetics and Tree Improvement, Forest Pest Management, and Soil Session at the Society of American Foresters National Convention,* held at San Francisco on Aug. 4-7, 1991.

Schwantes, Carlos A.
    1985   *Coxey's army: an American odyssey.* Lincoln: University of Nebraska Press. 321 pp.
    1991   *In mountain shadows: a history of Idaho.* Lincoln: University of Nebraska Press. 292 pp.
    1993   *Railroad signatures across the Pacific Northwest.* Seattle: University of Washington Press. 360 pp.

Schwennesen, Don
    1993   Environmentalists decry Champion sale. *Missoulian,* July 21, 1993.
    1993   No changes, no job cuts, Crown Pacific reassures. *Missoulian,* Sept. 11, 1993, p.A1.

Schwinden, Theodore
    1950   *The Northern Pacific land grants in Congress.* Unpublished B.A. thesis. Missoula: Montana State University (now University of Montana). 132 pp.

Seattle Daily Journal of Commerce
    1990   Plum Creek/Sumitomo plant opens with a gala ceremony: Spokane's 1st U.S./Japanese joint venture. Feb. 19, 1990.
    1990   Groups lobby against log ban. Feb. 21, 1990.

Seattle Post-Intelligencer
    1988   Trees, owls and schools. Editorial, March 4, 1988.
    1988   Burlington Resources subsidiary reports big lode near Salmon, Idaho. Nov. 30, 1988.
    1993   State log export ban. Editorial, May 16, 1993.
    1993   Burlington Resources to offer trusts. June 14, 1993, p. B5.
    1993   Plum Creek buys timberlands. July 20, 1993, p. B5.

Seattle Times
    1990   Study claims log ban would reduce jobs. Jan. 5, 1990.
    1993   SPO Partners buys stake in Plum Creek. Jan. 4, 1993, p. F5.
    1993   Court kills export ban on state's logs: appeals panel says federal law to aid small mills is unconstitutional. May 5, 1993, pp. A1,A3.

1993   How your U.S. lawmaker voted (forest land). May 23, 1993, p. A6.

1993   Plum Creek to buy Montana land from Champion. July 20, 1993, p. D3.

Selcraig, Bruce
1990   The secrets of Gray Ranch. *New York Times Magazine,* June 3, 1990, pp.28-34, 52-54.

Selden, Ron
1990   Researchers want bear facts: study might answer grizzly questions. *Missoulian,* June 6, 1990. Reprinted in *Transitions,* April 1992, p.16.

Servheen, Christopher
1992   *Grizzly bear recovery plan.* Second review draft. U.S. Fish & Wildlife Service, June 1992.

Severson, Kim and Elizabeth Moore
1990   The rush to cut: private forests losing ground to timber company saws. *Tacoma News Tribune,* May 27, 1990. Reprinted in *Transitions,* March 1991, p.17-19.

Sher, Jeff
1986   St. Joe River clearcut criticized: Plum Creek's activities under fire from environmentalists, Forest Service. *Spokesman-Review,* Aug. 17, 1986. Reprinted in *Transitions,* April 1992, pp.28-29.

1986   Plum Creek Timber Co. accused of overcutting. *Spokesman-Review,* Sept. 22, 1986. Reprinted in *Transitions,* April 1992, pp.30-31.

Simon, Jim
1990   Log-export limit faces legal test: resources board defies governor. *Seattle Times,* Sept. 5, 1990, pp.B1, B4.

Simonsen, William
    1992   Anti-Williams memo sent with Plum Creek checks. *Bigfork Eagle*, Sept. 30, 1992. Reprinted in *Transitions*, Sept./Oct. 1994, pp. 43-44.

Sinclair, Andrew
    1981   *Corsair: the life of J. Pierpont Morgan.* Boston: Little, Brown & Co. 269 pp.

Skille, Jack
    1991   In-stream sediment and fish populations in the Little North Fork Clearwater River, Shoshone and Clearwater Counties, Idaho 1988-90. *Water Quality Summary Report No. 27.* Coeur d'Alene: Idaho Department of Health and Welfare, Division of Environmental Quality. 18 pp.

Smalley, Eugene V.
    1883   *History of the Northern Pacific Railroad.* New York: G.P. Putnam's Sons. Arno Press, 1975 reprint. 437 pp.

Sobel, Robert
    1988   *Panic on Wall Street.* New York: E.P. Dutton. 531 pp.

Society of American Foresters
    1989   *Report of the Society of American Forests National Task Force on Community Stability.* SAF Resource Policy Series. Bethesda, Maryland: SAF, 1989. 42 pp.

Sommers, Paul and Helen Birss
    1990   *Revitalizing the timber dependent regions of Washington.* Seattle: University of Washington, Graduate School of Public Affairs, Northwest Policy Center. 179 pp. plus appendices.

Sonner, Scott
    1990   Timber industry trying to unite. *Seattle Daily Journal of Commerce,* Sept. 11, 1990.
    1991   Dissenters' fate turns focus on FS. *Missoulian,* Sept. 8, 1991. Reprinted in *Transitions,* Dec. 1991, pp.28-29.

1992 "Phantom forests" skewing harvests. *Journal American* (Bellevue, Wash.), June 16, 1992.

1992 Study: padded figures pushed timber quotas above capacity. *Lewiston Morning Tribune,* June 16, 1992.

1993 Murray seeks to restore raw-log ban. *Seattle Times,* May 7, 1993, p.C2.

Spencer, Hal
1990 Gardner aide, drafting log-export bans, assails Boyle: land commissioner asks changes; his staff called 'surly, uncooperative.' *Seattle Times,* Nov. 7, 1990, p.D3.

Spokane Chronicle
1930 Claim millions of acres of U.S. land wrongfully held; Government makes allegations against Northern Pacific. Aug. 1, 1930. Reprinted in *Transitions,* March, 1992, pp. 15, 17.

Spokesman-Review
1907 Forest millions saved to nation. March 8, 1907. Reprinted in *Transitions,* June 1992, p. 35.

1908 Roosevelt and 44 governors sit; in council with them are statesmen and jurists; labor chiefs, too; engineers and captains of industry join in momentous conference; for weal of nation; how best to husband natural resources of country to be planned; address by president; Andrew Carnegie and John Michelt also warn people of waste of soil's riches, May 14, 1908. Reprinted in *Transitions,* June 1992, p.37.

1930 N.P. land grant account asked; United States sues in Spokane court to quiet titles worth millions. Aug. 1, 1930. Reprinted in *Transitions,* March, 1992, pp.15.

1992 Boise Cascade eyes deal with Russians. June 26, 1992. Reprinted in *Transitions,* July 1992, p.85.

St. Clair, Jeffrey
1991 The Lolo goes solo. *Forest Watch* 12(3): 12-14, Oct. 13, 1991.

St. Clair, Jeffrey and Scott Greacen
1991   Calm in the eye of the storm: how the Lolo dropped the cut. *Forest Watch* 12(3): 15-17, Oct. 13, 1991.

St. Paul Pioneer Press
1900   Deal now closed: the Weyerhaeuser syndicate pays Northern Pacific $6,500,000. Jan. 3, 1900. Reprinted in *Transitions,* Feb. 1992, p.33.

Steen, Harold K.
1969   *Forestry in Washington to 1925.* Ph.D. thesis. Seattle: University of Washington.
1991   *The U.S. Forest Service: a history.* Seattle: University of Washington Press. 356 pp.

Strickland, Daryl
1992   Weyerhaeuser carves deal: pact calls for purchase of 5 mills, timberland. *Seattle Times,* Aug. 20, 1992, p.B1.

Stryker, Lisa
1989   Forest Service employee criticizes agency's ethics. *Register Guard* (Eugene, Oregon), June 3, 1989.

Summerfield, Bob
1985   *Woodland caribou cumulative effects analysis model.* Working draft. Coeur d'Alene: U.S. Forest Service, Idaho Panhandle National Forests.

Swisher, Larry
1990   Exporters fighting ban idea: no shortage of logs, timber interests say. *Register Guard* (Eugene, Oregon), March 2, 1990. Reprinted in *Transitions,* May 1992, p.17.

Tapperson, Trask
1992   Trillium makes major buy. *Bellingham Herald,* June 16, 1992, p. A1-A2.

Taylor, Rob
1990   Log export curbs 'simple, wrong,' Weyerhaeuser says. *Seattle Post-Intelligencer,* Oct. 11, 1990, p.B2.

1992   State adopts tighter restrictions on logging. *Seattle Post-Intelligencer,* June 27, 1992, p.B1.

1993   Forest plot in danger: Greenway link may fall victim to logging. *Seattle Post-Intelligencer,* April 19, 1993.

Taylor, A.L. and E.D. Forsman
1976   Recent range extensions of the barred owl in western America, including the first records for Oregon. *Condor* 78: 560-561.

Taylor, Rob and Larry Werner
1990   Worried Weyerhaeuser chief insists: 'we do care.' *Seattle Post-Intelligencer,* Nov. 10, 1990, pp.A1, A4, A5.

Thomas, K.R.
1989   *Regulation of timber exports: options.* Report for Congress. Washington, D.C.: U.S. Congressional Research Service.

1990   Plum Creek's chainsaw massacre. *Business & Society Review* 75: 43-47, Fall 1990.

Thompson, Steve
1990   Mudslide infuriates neighbors of clearcut. *Idahonian,* June 1, 1990. Reprinted in *Transitions,* July 1990, p.6.

Titone, Julie
1990   Export ban support builds: mills, activists want raw logs to stay in U.S. *Spokesman-Review,* May 1, 1990. Reprinted in *Transitions,* May 1990, p.4.

1990   Company specializes in placing public land on the trading block; trader's ultimate goal: consolidating National Forests. *Spokesman-Review,* July 29, 1990.

1991   Activists hoping law will curb timber firm. *Spokesman-Review,* March 10, 1991. Reprinted in *Transitions,* May 1992, p.20.

1991   Plum Creek can bid on area timber. *Spokesman-Review ,* April 18, 1991. Reprinted in *Transitions,* May 1992, p.21.

Twining, Charles E.
  1985   *Phil Weyerhaeuser: lumberman.* Seattle: University of
          Washington Press. 401 pp.

Ulrich, Alice H.
  1988   U.S. timber production, trade, consumption, and price
          statistics 1950-86. *Miscellaneous Publication No. 1460.*
          Washington, D.C.: U.S. Forest Service, June 1988. 81 pp.
  1990   U.S. timber production, trade, consumption, and price
          statistics 1960-88. *Miscellaneous Publication No. 1486.*
          Washington, D.C.: U.S. Forest Service, Dec. 1990. 80 pp.

UPI (United Press International)
  1990   Private timber falling rapidly. *Ellensburg, Washington
          Daily Record,* April 12, 1990.

U.S. Bureau of Corporations
  1913-14 *The lumber industry.* Study done by the U.S. Dept. of
          Commerce and Labor, Bureau of Corporations, Joseph E.
          Davies Commission. Washington, D.C.: U.S. Government
          Printing Office. 4 parts in 3 volumes.

U.S. Bureau of the Census
  1973   *Historical statistics of the United States: colonial times to
          1970.* U.S. House Document No.93-78, 93rd Cong., 1st
          sess. Washington, D.C.: U.S. Dept. of Commerce, Bureau
          of the Census. 2 vols.

U.S. Congress
  1924-28 *Hearings, the Northern Pacific land grants.* Joint
          Congressional Committee on the Investigation of the
          Northern Pacific Railroad Land Grants. Washington, D.C.:
          U.S. Goverment Printing Office. 15 parts. Superintendent
          of Documents No. Y4.N81:H35.

U.S. Fish & Wildlife Service
  1991-92 Critical habitat designation proposals for the northern
          spotted owl. Published in the *Federal Register* on May 6,
          1991, Aug. 13, 1991, and Jan. 1992.

U.S. Forest Service

1923 *Forest figures for the Pacific Coast states.* Jointly compiled and endorsed by the state, private, and federal agencies in California, Oregon, Washington, Idaho and Montana for the Senate Select Committee on Reforestation. Printed by the Western Forestry and Conservation Association.

1963 *Timber trends in western Oregon and western Washington.* Portland, Oregon: U.S. Forest Service, Pacific Northwest Forest & Range Experiment Station.

1979 *IPNF Planning Document 0882.* Letter from district ranger R.O. Brogden to Forest Supervisor regarding forest land use planning process, checkerboard ownership, June 19, 1979. Forest planning files, IPNF supervisor's office, Coeur d'Alene, Idaho.

1981 *IPNF Planning Document 0892.* Letter from Roy Swords, Landownership Adjustment Specialist, to Forest Supervisor. Jan. 22, 1981. Forest planning files, IPNF supervisor's office, Coeur d'Alene, Idaho.

1982 *IPNF Planning Document 1775.* Letter from Avery District Ranger, Denis Hart, to Forest Supervisor. March 30, 1982. Forest planning files, IPNF supervisor's office, Coeur d'Alene, Idaho.

1986 *IPNF Planning Document 1699.* Letter dated Feb. 26, 1986. District Ranger M.A. Dumas to Forest Supervisor regarding forest plan ground truthing harvest schedules. Forest planning files, IPNF supervisor's office, Coeur d'Alene, Idaho.

1986 *IPNF Planning Document 1690.* IPNF Final Plan Development (May 2, 1986, Idaho team recommendation to management team). Forest planning files, IPNF supervisor's office, Coeur d'Alene, Idaho.

1986 *IPNF Planning Document 1710* "Yellow" paper. Avery Ranger District. Forest planning files, IPNF supervisor's office, Coeur d'Alene, Idaho.

1992 Memo regarding ecosystem management and reduction of clearcutting. Washington, D.C., June 4, 1992.

U.S. Forest Service and Bureau of Land Management
    1990   *Actions the administration may wish to consider in implementing a conservation strategy for the northern spotted owl*, May 1, 1990. 52 pp.

U.S. General Accounting Office
    1991   *Forest Service timber harvesting, planting, assistance programs and tax provisions.* GAO/RCED-90-107BR. Washington, D.C.: U.S. GAO, April 1990. 19 pp.

U.S. General Services Administration
    1963   *Inventory report on real property owned by the United States throughout the world, as of June 30, 1963.* Washington, D.C.: U.S. General Services Administration.

U.S. House Committee on Interior and Insular Affairs
    1992   *Management of federal timber resources: the loss of accountability.* Compiled by the staff of the Committee on Interior and Insular Affairs, U.S. House of Representatives, Washington, D.C., June 15, 1992. 29 pp.

U.S. Interstate Commerce Commission
    1977   *Railroad conglomerates & other corporate structures: a report to congress as directed by section 903 of the railroad revitalization and regulatory reform act of 1976.* Washington, D.C.: U.S. ICC, Feb. 5, 1977. 82pp. plus appendices.

U.S. Senate
    1933   *A national plan for American forestry.* Sen. Doc. 12, 73d Cong., 1st sess., March 13, 1933. (The "Copeland Report.")

Van der Kamp, Bart J.
    1991   Pathogens as agents of diversity in forested landscapes. *The Forestry Chronicle* 67(4): 353-354, Aug. 1991.

Van Hooser, Dwane D. and Alan W. Green
   1985   Idaho's state and private forest resource. *Resource Bulletin INT-37.* Ogden, Utah: U.S. Forest Service, Intermountain Research Station. 78 pp.

Virgin, Bill
   1991   State hopes to carve out new wood markets. *Seattle Post-Intelligencer,* June 27, 1991.
   1992   Weyerhaeuser is hit hard, plans closures. *Seattle Post-Intelligencer,* Jan. 4, 1992, pp.A1-A2.
   1992   California group interested in 10 percent of Plum Creek. *Seattle Post-Intelligencer,* Oct. 3, 1992.
   1993   Burlington sells off Plum Creek shares. *Seattle Post-Intelligencer,* Jan. 5, 1993.
   1993   Burlington Resources keeps cooking with gas. *Seattle Post-Intelligencer,* March 20, 1993, p.B4.

Vlosky, Richard P. and Jay Gruenfeld
   1985   The history of North American West Coast log exports and a comment on the future of log exports from Alaska. *Alaska Forest Market Report,* June 1985. 7 pp.

Waddell, Karen L. et al.
   1989   Forest statistics of the United States, 1987. *Resource Bulletin PNW-RB-168.* Portland, Oregon: U.S. Forest Service, Pacific Northwest Research Station, Sept. 1989. 106 pp.

Wall Street Journal
   1990   Logging on protectionism. Sept. 6, 1990, p. A14.

Wallace, Henry A.
   1933   A national plan for American forestry: letter from the Secretary of Agriculture to the President of the United States, March 27, 1933. Reprinted in *Transitions,* March 1991, pp.9-11.
   1940   Letter written to the *Seattle Post-Intelligencer* and published as "Wallace analyzes forest problems: urges

Northwest to lock barn door 'before timber horse is stolen.' " Aug. 25, 1940. Reprinted in *Transitions,* March 1991, pp.12-16.

Warren, Debra D.
1991   Production, prices, employment, and trade in Northwest forest industries, first quarter 1991. *Resource Bulletin PNW-RB-188.* Portland, Oregon: U.S. Forest Service, Pacific Northwest Research Station, Oct. 1991. 112 pp.
1992   Production, prices, employment, and trade in Northwest forest industries, first quarter 1992. *Resource Bulletin PNW-RB-193.* Portland, Oregon: U.S. Forest Service, Pacific Northwest Research Station, Sept. 1992. 116 pp.
1994   Production, prices, employment, and trade in Northwest forest industries, fourth quarter 1993. Resource Bulletin PNW-RB-202. Portland,Oregon: U.S. Forest Service, Pacific northwest Research Station, May 1994.

Washington State Employment Security Division
1990   *Impacts on employment of timber supply decline.* Olympia: The Division.

Washington State Office of Financial Management
1991   *1989-91 Washington State biennial report on state agencies.* Olympia: Washington State OFM, Oct. 1991.

Weisbrod, A.R.
1976   Insularity and mammal species numbers in two national parks. Pages 83-87 in: *Proceedings of the 1st Conference on Scientific Research in the National Parks.* Edited by R.M. Linn. U.S. National Park Service, Transactions and Proceedings, Series 5.

Welch, James with Paul Stekler
1994   *Killing Custer.* New York: W.W. Norton and Co. 320pp.

Western Wood Products Association
1992   *1991 Statistical yearbook of the Western lumber industry,* Portland, Oregon: WWPA. 33pp.

Weyerhaeuser

1975   *Innovations and trees: Weyerhaeuser 1900-1975.* Booklet published for the company's 75th anniversary.

1990   Form 10-K, 1990. Filed with the U.S. Securities and Exchange Commission.

1990   1990 Annual Report. Tacoma, Washington: Weyerhaeuser Co.

1990   We can have both forests and forest-based economic opportunities in Washington: forever, if we manage all our resources wisely. *Seattle Times,* July 17, 1990, p.F8. Full-page advertisement.

1990   Weyerhaeuser has about 1.6 million acres of forestland in Washington; right now, 98% of it is growing trees. *Seattle Post-Intelligencer,* July 24, 1990. Full-page advertisement.

1990   We aren't running out of trees. Not here. Not now. Not ever. *Seattle Post-Intelligencer,* Aug. 7, 1990, p.B3. Full-page advertisement.

1991   Form 10-Q, June 1991. Filed with the U.S. Securities and Exchange Commission.

1991   At loggerheads over exports. *Weyerhaeuser Today,* Nov./ Dec. 1991. 4 page supplement.

White, W. Thomas

1984   Railroad labor protests, 1894-1917. *Pacific Northwest Quarterly,* Jan. 1984, pp. 13-21.

Wicker, Tom

1989   Deforestation of the United States only benefits Japan. *New York Times.* (Date unavailable.)

1989   Log-export scheme ill-conceived. *Spokesman-Review,* March 22, 1989.

Wickman, Boyd E.

1992   Letter to Dr. Thomas Lawson of Lawson-Rasor Associates, Aug. 25, 1992, in possession of John Osborn, Inland Empire Public Lands Council.

Wilhelm, Steve
    1991   Ports feel the squeeze from drop in log exports. *Puget Sound Business Journal,* July 29, 1991, p.16.

Williams, James M.
    1989   Access to the Gallatin National Forest: a case study. *Transactions of the 54th North American Wildlife and Natural Resources Conference,* pp.155-158.

Williams, Pat
    1989   Testimony before the U.S. Senate Subcommittee on International Finance and Monetary Affairs, Committee on Banking, Housing, and Urban Affairs, Nov. 7, 1989.

Wilner, Frank N.
    1981   History and evolution of railroad land grants. *ICC Practitioners Journal* 48(6): 687-699, Sept./Oct. 1981.

Winkler, John K.
    1930   *Morgan the magnificent.* Balboa Park, Massachusets: Spear & Staff. 313 pp.

Winks, Robin
    1991   *Frederick Billings.* New York: Oxford University Press. 398 pp.

Wisdom, M.J., L.R. Bright, C.G. Carey, et al.
    1986   *A model to evaluate elk habitat in western Oregon.* Portland, Oregon: U.S. Forest Service.

Woodruff, Steve
    1985   Report warns of depletion of private timber. *Missoulian,* Dec. 10, 1985.
    1989   Plum Creek throws down the gauntlet. *Missoulian,* May 28, 1989. Reprinted in *Transitions,* May 1990, pp.19-22.

Wright, Gregory
    1990   Industry eyeing Soviet timber. *Missoulian,* June 22, 1990. Reprinted in *Transitions,* July 1992, p.85.

Yenne, Bill
   1991   *The history of the Burlington Northern.* New York: Bonanza Books. 128 pp.

INDEX

A

Adams, Brock   86
Amalgamated Copper Company   4, 28
American Fisheries Society   51
American Forestry Association   61
American Plywood Association   68
Anaconda Copper   4, 28
Anderson and Olson   66
Andrus, Cecil   94
Anez, Bob   69
Arikaris   102
Armstrong, Anne   36
AuCoin, Les   81

B

Baldwin, Pamela   96
Baucus, Max   21
Beecher, Henry Ward   9
Belcher, Jennifer   93
Benson, Fred   86
Billings, Frederick   12
Bingham, Charles   85
Blackfoot   102
Boeh, Bob   45
Boeing   78
Boise Cascade   25, 31, 35, 36, 37, 57, 66, 67, 68, 69, 75, 102
Boise Payette   4, 35
Boyle, Brian   44
Bressler, Richard   21
British Columbia   78
Burlington Northern   4, 7, 14, 21, 22-24, 26, 58, 92, 98, 99, 102, 104
Burlington Northern Railroad   15
Burlington Resources   4, 14, 23, 24, 26, 27, 29, 98, 99, 102
Burns, Conrad   81
Bush, George   77, 80

C

Canada   36, 43, 78, 87
Cascade Lumber   35
Champion International   4, 26, 28, 31, 45, 66, 67, 68, 69, 92
Chandler, Rod   86

INLAND EMPIRE
PUBLIC LANDS COUNCIL

T he Inland Empire Public Lands Council (the "Council") is dedicated to the transition of the greater Columbia River ecosystem from resource extraction to long-term community and biological sustainability. The Council will achieve its goal by increasing public awareness through education and promoting public participation in decision-making processes.

Begun in 1983 as the Spokane Resident Physicians Action League by the physician "house staff" at Sacred Heart and Deaconess Medical Centers in Spokane, Washington, the group changed its name in 1985 to Inland Empire Public Lands Council.

The Council publishes *Transitions*, a journal which chronicles the historic change underway in America's Pacific Northwest.

The Council's Forest Watch Program, started in 1990, has organized and trained 20 grassroots groups on 29 ranger districts in nine National Forests in the four states of the Pacific Northwest. The purpose of Forest Watch is to provide citizen oversight of the federal government's decisions about forests.

With the assistance of the Sierra Club Legal Defense Fund, the Council established the Public Lands Legal Program in 1994. The program provides local citizen groups with legal advice and litigation support.

The Council's public outreach program has helped hundreds of volunteers take the message of forest destruction door-to-door in the neighborhoods of eastern Washington and north Idaho, and alerted the public through billboards, busboards, radio, and newspapers.

After nearly a decade of research and documentation of forest destruction, the Council is restoring Congress's 1864 Northern Pacific railroad land grant – neglected for nearly half a century – to the attention of the American people, where the issue belongs.

Inland Empire Public Lands Council
P.O. Box 2174 • Spokane, WA 99210
Phone: (509) 838-4912 • Fax: (509) 838-5155
Internet: IEPLC@uwsa.spk.wa.us

ABOUT THE AUTHORS

DERRICK JENSEN

Derrick Jensen received a Bachelor of Science in Mineral Engineering Physics from the Colorado School of Mines in 1983 and a Master of Fine Arts in Creative Writing from Eastern Washington University in 1992. He is the author of the book *Listening to the Land: Nature, Culture, and Eros*, to be published by Sierra Club Books in spring of 1995.

GEORGE DRAFFAN

George Draffan received a Bachelor's degree in History from the University of Oregon and a Master's degree in Librarianship from the University of Washington. He has worked as a research librarian for the U.S. Forest Service and other public agencies, law firms, private companies, public interest organizations, and labor unions. He is a founding board member of the Greater Ecosystem Alliance and the Institute on Trade Policy.

JOHN OSBORN, M.D.

John Osborn received a combined Bachelor's degree in History, Zoology, and Human Ecology from Albertson College of Idaho in Caldwell, Idaho, in 1979; graduated from the University of Washington School of Medicine in 1983; and completed his Internal Medicine residency in Spokane, Washington, in 1986. He is a staff physician with the Veterans Medical Center in Spokane and heads programs in AIDS and medical ethics. Osborn worked as a firefighter and in recreation for the Forest Service during summers from 1974 until 1980. In 1983 he founded the Spokane Resident Physicians Action League (now the Inland Empire Public Lands Council); serves on the boards of the Idaho Conservation League, the Idaho Wildlife Federation, and the Washington Wilderness Coalition; and is conservation chair for the Sierra Club's Northern Rockies chapter.